How to Start & Manage
A Home Attendent Service Business

Lewis & Renn Associates, Inc.

Business & Professional Publishing

10315 Harmony Drive
Interlochen, Michigan 49643
(231) 275-7287

Leslie D. Renn
President

Jerre G. Lewis
Secretary-Treasurer

ISBN # 978-1-57916-178-1
Library of Congress Catalog Card Number
99-094175

TABLE OF CONTENTS

Chapter 1

Introduction

Selecting the right Home Attendant business opportunity requires careful, thorough evaluations of yourself. Owning your own business is as much a part of the American dream as owning a home, and for you, this urge represents one of life's most exciting challenges. This book is for those men and women who someday may go into business for themselves and for those who are already in business for themselves but wish to strengthen their entrepreneurial and managerial skills.

Entrepreneurs come in all shapes and sizes, personalities, and lifestyles. They are usually highly motivated, hard-working individuals who receive satisfaction from taking risks. Your business should interest you, not just be an income generator. Analyze your personal style. Do you like working with people? Are you a self starter, goal oriented, persistent, a risk taker, willing to work hard and long hours?

If you have been honest in evaluating yourself, you will now select the right type of business. Before you can determine which of the multitude of businesses is right for you to start, you must evaluate the businesses you want to start by asking these questions. Is the business area growing? How does the economy affect it? Who dominates its market? Once you have considered a business that satisfies your needs and interest you must prepare a formal business plan by following the outline given in this book.

Small businesses constitute a dynamic and critical sector of the U.S. economy. Every year in the United States more than 600,000 new businesses are launched by independent men and women eager to make their own decisions, express their own ideas, and be their own bosses. But running your own business is not as easy as it may seem. There can be problems with the inventory, or getting the right goods delivered on time. Yet, managing one's own business can be a personally and financially rewarding experience for an individual strong enough to meet the test. A person with stamina, maturity, and creativity, one who is willing to make sacrifices, may find making a go of a struggling enterprise an exhilarating challenge with many compensations.

Small business owners are a dedicated group of people who work hard and whose hours on the job usually exceed the nine-to-five routine. The owner's commitment is the key to many successful small businesses; an entrepreneur is able to communicate ideas, lead, plan, be patient, and work well with people.

Managing a business requires more than the possession of technical knowledge. Because most small businesses are started by technical people, such as engineers and salesmen, their managerial acumen is often less developed than their technical skills. The need to plan for management is common to every type of and size of business, and there are certain steps that must be taken. Although some of them are very elementary — such as applying for a city business permit — the most important are often complex and difficult and require the advice of specialists: accountants, attorneys, insurance brokers, and/or bankers. For almost any business though, the first step will be to translate the entrepreneur's basic idea into a concrete plan for action.

To gauge your level of entrepreneurial spirit, the following quiz was created. Please answer each question honestly and then total the columns.

ENTREPRENEURIAL QUIZ

	YES	NO	SOMETIMES
1. I am a self-starter. Nobody has to tell me how to get going.	____	____	_____
2. I am capable of getting along with just about everybody.	____	____	_____
3. I have no trouble getting people to follow my lead.	____	____	_____
4. I like to be in charge of things and see them through.	____	____	_____
5. I always plan ahead before beginning a project. I am usually the one who gets everyone organized.	____	____	_____
6. I have a lot of stamina. I can keep going as long as necessary.	____	____	_____
7. I have no trouble making decisions and can make up my mind in a hurry.	____	____	_____
8. I say exactly what I mean. People can trust me.	____	____	_____
9. Once I make my mind up to do something, nothing can stop me.	____	____	_____
10. I am in excellent health and have a lot of energy.	____	____	_____

	YES	NO	SOMETIMES

11. I have experience or
technical knowledge in
the business I intend to
start.

12. I feel comfortable taking
risks if it is something
I really believe in.

13. I have good communication
skills.

14. I am flexible in my dealings
with people and situations.

15. I consider myself creative
and resourceful.

16. I can analyze a situation
and take steps to correct
problems.

17. I think I am capable of
maintaining a good
working relationship
with employees.

18. I am not a dictator.
I am willing to listen to
employees, customers
and suppliers.

19. I am not rigid in my policies.
I am willing to adjust to
meet the needs of employees,
customers, and suppliers.

20. More than anything else,
I want to run my own
business.

Total of Column #1   _____

Total of Column #2   _____

Total of Column #3   _____

If the total of Column #1 is the highest, then you will probably be very successful in running your own business.

If the total of Column #2 is the highest, you may find that running a business is more than you can handle.

If the total of Column #3 is the highest, you should consider taking on a partner who is strong in your weak areas.

NOTE: This quiz was adapted from the Small Business Administration publication *Checklist for Going Into Business.*

*Notes*_____

Chapter 2

Planning the Business

The Dream of self-employment can be fulfilled. You don't need to finance the opening of an elaborate office or facility to start your own one-person corporation either. You can start your own Home Attendant Business.

Anyone preparing to run an Home Attendant Business needs to learn a great deal to assure the best possible chance for success.

GETTING STARTED

The following is a list of what you need to accomplish to insure that your Home Attendant endeavor will head in the right direction.

1. Define your educational background and work experience.

2. Survey all the basic types of Home Attendant businesses.

3. Define what products or services your Home Attendant Business will be marketing.

4. Define who will be using your products/services.

5. Define why they will be purchasing your products/services.

6. List all competitors in your Home Attendant marketing area.

ZONING REGISTRATIONS

Home Attendant businesses are subject to many laws and regulations enforced by state, county, township governmental units. Most jurisdictions now have codes, a zoning board, and an appeal board which regulate businesses. Areas often are zoned residential, commercial or industrial.

You must become familiar with these regulations. If you are doing business in violation of these regulations, you could be issued a cease and desist order or fined.

Certain kinds of goods cannot be produced in the home, though these restrictions vary somewhat from state-to-state. Most states outlaw home production of fireworks, drugs, poisons, explosives, sanitary/medical products and some toys.

Many localities have registration requirements for new businesses. You will need to obtain a work certificate or license from the state.

TAX REQUIREMENTS

<u>Application for Employer Identification Number</u>, Form SS-4. This registers you with the Internal Revenue Service as a business. If you have employees, you should ask for Circular E along with your ID number. Circular E explains federal income and social security tax withholding requirements.

<u>Employer's Annual Unemployment Tax Return</u>, Form 940. This is only if you have employees. It's used to report and pay the Federal Unemployment Compensation Tax.

<u>Employee's Withholding Allowance Certificate</u>, W-4. Every employee must complete the W-4 so the proper amount of income tax can be withheld from the

employee's pay. If the employee claims more than 15 allowances or a complete withholding exemption while having a salary of more than $200 a week, a copy of the W-4 must go to the IRS.

Employer's Wage and Tax Statement, W-2. Used to report to the IRS the total taxes withheld and total compensation paid to each employee per year.

Reconciliation/Transmittal of Income and Tax Statements, W-3. Used to total all information from the W-2. Sent to the Social Security Administration.

The IRS puts on monthly workshops on understanding and using these forms. Call your local IRS office for further information.

States also have various tax form requirements including: an unemployment tax form, a certificate of registration application, a sales and use tax return, an employer's quarterly contribution and payroll report, an income tax withholding registration form, an income tax withholding form, and others. Some forms apply only to employers who have employees. Your local IRS office and state Office of Taxation can provide you with listings of forms you will need to start your business. The following table outlines Federal tax form requirements.

Every small business begins with an idea — a product to be manufactured or sold, a service to be performed.

Whatever the business or its degree of complexity, the owner needs a business plan in order to transform a vision into a working operation.

This business plan should describe in writing and in figures the proposed Home Attendant business and its products, services, or manufacturing processes. It should also include an analysis of the market, a marketing strategy, an organizational plan, and measurable financial objectives.

WHAT SHOULD A BUSINESS PLAN COVER?

It should be a thorough and objective analysis of both personal abilities and business requirements for a particular product or service. It should define strategies for such functions as marketing and production, organization and legal aspects, accounting and finance. A business plan should answer such questions as:

What do I want and what am I capable of doing?

What are the most workable ways of achieving my goals?

What can I expect in the future?

There is no single best way to begin. What follows is simply a guide and can be changed to suit individual needs.

1. Define Long-term goals.
2. State short-term.
3. Set marketing strategies to meet goals and objectives.
4. Analyze available resources.
5. Assemble financial data.
6. Review plan.

Please refer to Figure 2.1 for a complete business plan outline.

The business operator with a realistic plan has the best chance for success.

Figure 2.1

BUSINESS PLAN FOR SMALL BUSINESSES

I. Type of Business

II. Location

III. Target Market

IV. Planning Process

V. Organizational Structure

VI. Staffing Procedures

VII. Market Strategy

IX. Financial Planning

X. Budgeted Balance Sheet

XI. Budgeted Income Statement

XII. Budgeted Cash Flow Statement

XIII. Break-Even Chart

Notes _____

Chapter 3

Marketing Strategies
for an Home Attendant Business

As a potential Home Attendant business owner, it is important to learn all you can about marketing. You will need to know how to identify your market and how to market your product or service.

As a business person who looks for a profit from the sale of goods, you recognize that without people who want to buy, there is no demand for the things you want to sell. Thus, it is important that, in addition to knowing about the functions of marketing, you also study the activities that will influence the consumer. When you satisfy the specific needs and wants of the customer, then he or she may be willing to pay you a price that will include a profit for you — and to make a profit is one of the reasons you have become an Home Attendant Business owner. Although there are many activities connected with marketing, most of them can be classified in these categories: buy, finance, transport, standardize, store, insure, advertise and sell.

Target Market Analysis

Before you can create a successful marketing campaign, it's necessary to determine your target market (toward whom to direct your energies). The whole concept of target marketing can seem very scary at first. On the surface, targeting appears to be limiting the scope of the pool of potential customers. Many people fear that by defining a market, they will lose business. They are concerned that they will choose the wrong market. Or that other practitioners will take just anybody and therefore some of their business.

You must keep in mind that the purpose of defining your target market is to make your life easier and increase the productivity of your promotional endeavors. Many opportunities exist in this world and it's impossible to pursue them all or be everything to everyone. You need to know where to focus your energy and money when it comes to promotion and advertising.

The two most common means of market analysis are demographics and psychographics, which describe a person in terms of objective data and personality attributes.

Demographics are statistics such as:
- age
- gender
- income level
- geographic location
- occupation
- education level

Psychographics are lifestyle factors including:
- special interest activities
- philosophical beliefs
- social factors
- cultural involvements

The more you know about your potential customers, the easier it is to develop an appropriate position statement and design an effective marketing campaign. The actual number of target markets you have depends mainly upon the size of your practice and the scope of your knowledge.

Your Target Market Profile

In order to clarify your target market(s) you need to delineate the demographic and psychographic factors and then identify the characteristics your customers have in common.

Describe your current customers and those who are most likely your future customers:

What is the age range and average age of your customers?

What is the percentage of males?

What is the percentage of females?

What is the average educational level of your customers?

Where do your customers live?

What are the occupations of your customers?

Where do your customers work?

What is the average annual income level of your customers?

Of what special interest groups are your customers members?

What is the primary reason your customers use your services?

Defining Your Target Market(s)

Write a descriptive statement for each of your target markets (refer to your "Target Market Profile"). Include a brief overview of the services you are providing to that group and a detailed analysis of the characteristics of the specific clientele.

Target Market 1:

Target Market 2:

Target Market 3:

Home Attendant Business Marketing

The foundation for creating a thriving customer base.

A. Overview

This section is about clarifying your beliefs and attitudes toward your profession and determining the image you wish to portray.

1. Describe the "character" that you want for your business. Depict the image you want to convey:

2. State your philosophy in regard to your business:

3. Describe your philosophy regarding your practice in business:

B. Customer Profile

This is a descriptive analysis of your current and potential customers — who they are, what their interests are, and where you can find them. Include each of your target markets.

1. Target Market 1:

2. Target Market 2:

3. Target Market 3:

C. Competition's Marketing Assessment

The first phase in planning your promotional campaign is appraising the competition. List each of your major competitors and describe the marketing strategies they utilize. Be certain to include where and how often they advertise.

1. Major Competitor 1:

2. Major Competitor 2:

3. Major Competitor 3:

4. Major Competitor 4:

5. Major Competitor 5:

6. Major Competitor 6:

Home Attendant marketing Planning

Outline for Marketing:

I. Produce/Service Concept
    A. Name of produce or service
    B. Descriptive characteristics of product or service
    C. Unit sales
    D. Analysis of market trends

II. Number of Customers in Market Area:
    A. Profile of customers
    B. Average customer expenditure
    C. Total market

III. Your Market Potential:
    A. Total market divided by competition
    B. Total market multiplied by percent who will buy your product

IV. Needs of Customers:
    A. Identification
    B. Pleasure
    C. Social approval
    D. Personal interest
    E. Price

V. Direct Marketing Sources:
    A. Trade magazines
    B. Trade associates
    C. Small Business Administration (SBA)
    D. Government publications
    E. Yellow Pages
    F. Marketing directories

VI. Customer Profile:
    A. Geographical
    B. Gender
    C. Age range
    D. Income brackets
    E. Occupation
    F. Educational level

Chapter 4

Promoting the Home Attendant Business

When a new business is opened, the owner must be prepared to publicize the business or its chance for success will be slim. Only a few businesses — such as those with a prime location, nationally known name, or a built-in clientele — can succeed without advertising to promote market awareness and stimulate sales.

The first purpose — promoting customer awareness — applies as much to established businesses as to newcomers.

In the Home Attendant Business, you will find it easier to retain old customers than to win new ones. When old customers move away from your area, or when their buying needs change, you need new customers to maintain your sales volume. If you expect your business to gain, you will need additional new customers. New customers are those who move into your area or who have grown into your line of products because now they can afford them or they need them. We see advertising and we hear advertising all around us, and yet that is only a part of it. Through advertising, you call the attention of customers to your products.

As a small business owner, you may advertise your business through your location. People pass by and are attracted to your operation because of what you are selling. To get a better idea of what advertising is, consider some of the following functions of advertising:

1. *To inform:* Letting customers know what you have for sale through brochures, leaflets, newspapers, radio, TV, and etc.

2. *Persuade:* Persuasion is the art of leading individuals to do what you want them to do. There are sales personnel who have persuasive sales presentations, but persuasion in advertising is nonpersonal. The appeal is made through the printed or spoken words or a picture. The influence of an ad on readers occurs as purchasers choose what they want among different products, and different wants. To gain the actions you want — <u>a sale</u> — you must persuade a customer to examine personally what you have for sale.

3. *Reminder:* Advertising performs it's third function when it reminds those who have been persuaded to buy once that the same product will bring satisfaction. The ad will also remind a customer of the characteristics of a product purchased some time ago, and where he or she bought it. Because customers change their loyalty to a place of business, their taste for products, and often their trading area patronage, advertising is necessary to draw new customers and to hold old customers. To generate results from advertising that will be profitable to your business, you will have to produce answers to the what, where and how of advertising.

What to Advertise

The nature of your business will partially answer the question "Shall I advertise goods or services?" What are the outstanding features of your business? Is it unique in any way? Does it have strong points? Do you have something to offer that the competition is not able to duplicate? Answers to these questions will give you a start in deciding what to advertise.

Where to Advertise

Of course, you will want to advertise within your marketing area, however there are a few guidelines to remember:

A. Who are your customers?

B. What is their income range?

C. Why do they buy?

D. How do they buy? Do they pay Cash? Charge?

E. What is the radius of your market area?

How to Advertise:

In determining how to advertise, you will have to consider your dollar allocation for advertising and the media suitable to your particular kind of business. However, it is important to have a balance between the presentation of the product or service being advertised and the application of three basic principles.

1. Gain the attention of the audience.

2. Establish a need.

3. Tell where that need may be filled.

See Figure A for an outline of the different advertising media and Figure B for budget on media goals.

Figure A

Advertising Media

Media	Market Coverage	Type of Audience
Daily Newspaper	Single community or entire metro area; zoned editions sometimes available	General
Weekly Newspaper	Single community	Residents
Telephone Directory	Geographical area or occupational field served by the directory	Active shoppers for goods or services
Direct mail audience	Controlled by the advertiser	Controlled
Radio audience	Definable market area	Selected
Television audience	Definable market area	Various
Outdoor	Entire metro area	General auto drivers
Magazine	Entire metro area or magazine region	Selected audience

Figure A

Promotion and Advertising Plan — Home Attendant Business

In designing your promotional plan, it's wise to use a variety of media. You must have specific goals, time lines and budgets for each marketing application

Media	Goal	Timeline	Budget

Notes _____

Chapter 5

Financial Planning for an
Home Attendant Business

Financial planning is the process of analyzing and monitoring the financial performance of your business so you can assess your current position and anticipate future problem areas. The daily, monthly, seasonal, and yearly operation of your business requires attention to the figures that tell you about the firm's financial health.

Maintaining good financial records is a necessary part of doing business.

The increasing number of governmental regulations alone makes it virtually impossible to avoid keeping detailed records. Just as important is to keep them for yourself. The success of your business depends on them. An efficient system of record keeping can help you to:

- make management decisions
- compete in the marketplace
- monitor performance
- keep track of expenses
- eliminate unprofitable merchandise
- protect your assets
- prepare your financial statements

Financial skills should include understanding of the balance sheet, the profit-and-loss statement, cash flow projection, break-even analysis, and source and application of funds. In many businesses, the husband and wife run the business; it is especially important that both of them understand financial management. Most small business owners are not accountants, but they must understand the tool of financial management if they are going to be able to measure the return on their investment. Although good records are essential to good financial planning, they alone are not enough because their full use requires interpretation and analysis. The owner/manager's financial decisions concerning return on invested funds, approaches to banks, securing greater supplier credit, raising additional equity capital and so forth, can be more successful if he takes the time to develop understanding and use of the balance sheet and profit-and-loss statement.

Balance Sheet:

The balance sheet, Figure I, shows the financial condition of a business at the end of business on a specific day. It is called a balance sheet because the total assets balance with, or are equal to, total liabilities plus owner's capital balance. Current assets are those that the owner does not anticipate holding for long. This category includes cash, finished goods in inventory, and accounts receivable. Fixed assets are long-term assets, including plant and equipment. A third possible category is the intangible asset of goodwill. Liabilities are debts owed by the business, including both accounts payable, which are usually short-term, and notes payable, which are usually long-term debts such as mortgage payments. The difference between the value of the assets and the value of the liabilities is the capital. This category includes funds invested by the owner plus accumulated profits, less withdrawals.

The Income Statement:

This statement, Figure II, is also known as a profit-and loss (P&L) statement. It shows how a business has performed over a certain period of time. An income statement specifies sales, costs of sales, gross profit, expenses and net income or loss from operations.

25

Figure I

Financial Forecast

Opening Balance Sheet - Date

ASSETS

Current Assets

Cash and bank accounts		$
Accounts receivable		$
Inventory		$
Other current assets		$ _____
TOTAL CURRENT ASSETS	(A)	$ _____

Fixed Assets

Property owned		$
Furniture and equipment		$
Business automobile		$
Leasehold improvements		$
Other fixed assets		$ _____
TOTAL FIXED ASSETS	(B)	$ _____
TOTAL ASSETS	(A+B = X)	$ _____

LIABILITIES

Current Liabilities (due within the next 12 months)

Bank loans		$
Other loans		$
Accounts payable		$
Other current liabilities		$ _____
TOTAL CURRENT LIABILITIES	(C)	$ _____

Long-term Liabilities

Mortgages		$
Long-term loans		$
Other long-term liabilities		$ _____
TOTAL LONG-TERM LIABILITIES	(D)	$ _____
TOTAL LIABILITIES	(C+D = Y)	$ _____
NET WORTH	(X-Y = Z)	$ _____
TOTAL NET WORTH AND LIABILITIES	(Y+Z)	$ _____

Figure II

Business Income and Expense Forecast for the Next 12 Months

One year estimate ending _____, 19 _____

Projected Number of Clients

For your services   _____

For your products   _____

TOTAL NUMBER OF CLIENTS   _____

Projected Income

Sessions $ _____

Product sales $ _____

Other $ _____

TOTAL INCOME $ _____

Projected Expenses

Start-up costs $ _____

Monthly expenses (x 12) $ _____

Annual expenses $ _____

TOTAL EXPENSES $ _____

TOTAL OPERATING PROFIT (OR LOSS) $ _____

CAPITAL REQUIRED FOR THE NEXT 12 MONTHS $ _____

Home Attendant Business

Start-Up Costs Worksheet	
Item	**Estimated Expense**
Open checking account	$
Telephone installation	$
Equipment	$
First & last month's rent, security deposit, etc.	$
Supplies	$
Business cards, stationery, etc.	$
Advertising and promotion package	$
Decorating and remodeling	$
Furniture and fixtures	$
Legal and professional fees	$
Insurance	$
Utility deposits	$
Beginning inventory	$
Installation of fixtures and equipment	$
Licenses and permits	$
Other	$
TOTAL	$

Fixed Annual Expense Worksheet	
Item	**Estimated Expense**
Property insurance	$
Business auto insurance	$
Licenses and permits	$
Liability insurance	$
Disability insurance	$
Professional society membership	$
Fees (legal, accounting, etc.)	$
Taxes	$
Other	$
TOTAL	$

Monthly Business Expense Worksheet		
Expense	**Estimated Monthly Cost**	**X 12**
Rent	$	$
Utilities	$	$
Telephone	$	$
Bank fees	$	$
Supplies	$	$
Stationery and business cards	$	$
Networking club dues	$	$
Education (seminars, books professional journals, etc.)	$	$
Business car (Payments, gas, repairs, etc)	$	$
Advertising and promotion	$	$
Postage	$	$
Entertainment	$	$
Repair, cleaning and maintenance	$	$
Travel	$	$
Business loan payments	$	$
Salary/Draw	$	$
Staff salaries	$	$
Miscellaneous	$	$
Taxes	$	$
Professional fees	$	$
Decorations	$	$
Furniture and fixtures	$	$
Equipment	$	$
Inventory	$	$
Other	$	$
TOTAL MONTHLY	$	$
TOTAL YEARLY		$

Cash Flow Forecast						
	January Estimate	January Actual	February Estimate	February Actual	March Estimate	March Actual
Beginning cash						
Plus monthly income from: Fees						
Sales						
Loans						
Other						
TOTAL CASH AND INCOME						
Expenses:						
Rent						
Utilities						
Telephone						
Bank fees						
Supplies						
Stationery and business cards						
Insurance						
Dues						
Education						
Auto						
Advertising and promotion						
Postage						
Entertainment						

Cash Flow Forecast (Continued)						
	January Estimate	January Actual	February Estimate	February Actual	March Estimate	March Actual
Repair and maintenance						
Travel						
Business loan payments						
Licenses and permits						
Salary/Draw						
Staff salaries						
Taxes						
Professional fees						
Decorations						
Furniture and fixtures						
Equipment						
Inventory						
Other Expenses						
TOTAL EXPENSES						
ENDING CASH (+/-)						

Notes _____

Chapter 6

Home Attendant Business Planning

Introduction

Our increasingly service oriented economy offers a widening spectrum of opportunities for customized and personalized small business growth. Though untrained entrepreneurs have traditionally had a high rate of failure, small businesses can be profitable. Success in a small Home Attendant Business is not an accident. It requires both skills in a service or product area and acquisition of management and attitudinal competencies.

The purpose of this publication is to help you take stock of your interests, aptitudes and skills. Many people have good business ideas but not everyone has what it takes to succeed. If you are convinced that a profitable Home Attendant Business is attainable, this publication will provide step-by-step guidance in development of the basic written business plan.

Information Gathering

A helpful tool for use in determining if you are ready to take the risks of an Home Attendant Business operation is the SMA publication entitled *Going Into Business* (MP-12).

It will help you focus on the basic steps in information gathering and business planning.

33

Careful planning is required to research legal and tax issues, proper space utilization and to establish time management discipline. Inadequate or careless attention to development of a detailed business plan can be costly for you and your family in terms of lost time, wasted talent and disappearing dollars.

The Entrepreneurial Personality

A variety of experts have documented research that indicates that successful small business entrepreneurs have some common characteristics. How do you measure up? On this checklist, write a "Y" if you believe the statement describes you; a "N" if it doesn't; and a "U" if you can't decide:

_____   I have a strong desire to be my own boss.

_____   Win lose or draw, I want to be master of my own financial destiny.

_____   I have significant specialized business ability based on both my education and my experience.

_____   I have an ability to conceptualize the whole of a business; not just its individual parts, but how they relate to each other.

_____   I develop an inherent sense of what is "right" for a business and have the courage to pursue it.

_____   One or both of my parents were entrepreneurs; calculate risk-taking runs in the family.

_____   My life is characterized by a willingness and capacity to preserver.

_____   I possess a high level of energy, sustainable over long hours to make the business successful.

While not every successful Home Attendant Business owner starts with a "Y" answer to all of these questions, three or four "N"s and "U"s should be sufficient reason for you to stop and give a second thought to going it alone. Many proprietors who sense entrepreneurial deficiencies seek extra training a support their limitations with help from a skilled team of business advisors such as accountants, bankers and attorneys.

Selecting a Business

A logical first step for the undecided is to list potential areas of personal background, special training, education and job experience, and special interests that could be developed into a business. Review the following list of activities which have proven marketable for others. On a scale of "0" (no interest or strength) to "10" (maximum interest or strength) indicate the potential for you and a total score for each activity.

Time Management

For both the novice and the experienced business person planning a small Home Attendant enterprise, an early concern requiring self-evaluation is time management.

It is very difficult for some people to make and keep work schedules even in a disciplined office setting. As your own boss the problem can be much greater. To determine how much time you can devote to your business, begin by drafting a weekly task timetable listing all current and potential responsibilities and the blocks of time required for each. When and how can business responsibilities be added without undue physical or mental stress on you or your family? Potential conflicts must be faced and resolved at the outset and as they occur, otherwise your business can become a nightmare. During the first year of operation, continue to chart, post and checkoff tasks on a daily, weekly and monthly basis.

Distractions and excuses for procrastination abound. It is important to keep both a planning and operating log. These tools will help avoid oversights and provide vital information when memory fails.

To improve the quality of work time, consider installation of a telephone line for the business and attaching an answering machine to take messages when you do not wish to be distracted or are away from your business. A business line has the added advantage of allowing you to have a business listing in the phone book and if you wish to buy it, an ad in the classified directory.

Is an Home Attendant Business Site Allowable?

Now you will want to investigate potential legal and community problems associated with operating the business. You should gather, read and digest specialized information concerning federal, state, county and municipal laws and regulations concerning Home Attendant Business operations.

Check first! Get the facts in writing. Keep a topical file for future reference. Some facts and forms will be needed for your business plan. There may be limitations enforced that can make your planned business impossible or require expensive modifications to your property.

Items to be investigated, recorded and studied are:

TO DO   DONE

_____   _____   county or city zoning code restrictions

_____   _____   necessary permits and licenses for operation

_____   _____   state and local laws and codes regarding zoning

_____   _____   deed or lease restrictions such as covenants and restrictive conditions of purchase

_____	_____	parking and customer access; deliveries
_____	_____	sanitation, traffic and noise codes
_____	_____	signs and advertising
_____	_____	state and federal code requirements for space, ventilation, heat and light
_____	_____	limitations on the number and type of workers. If not, check with the local Chamber of Commerce office
_____	_____	reservations that neighbors may have about a business next to or near them

Here are some ways to collect your information. Call or visit the zoning office at county headquarters or city hall. In some localities the city or county Office of Economic Development has print materials available to pinpoint key "code" items affecting a business.

Even in rural areas, the era of unlimited free enterprise is over. Although the decision makers may be in the state capital or in a distant regional office of a federal agency, check before investing in inventory, equipment or marketing programs. If in doubt, call the state office of Industrial Development or the nearest SBA district office. In some states the county agent or home demonstration agent will have helpful information concerning rural or farm business development.

Is the Business Site Insurable?

In addition to community investigations, contact your insurance company or agent. It is almost certain that significant changes will be required in your coverage and limits when you start a business. When you have written a good description of your business, call your agent for help in insuring you properly against new hazards resulting from your business operations such as:

- Fire, theft and casualty damage to inventories and equipment
- business interruption coverage
- fidelity bonds for employees
- liability for customers, vendors and others visiting the business
- workmen's compensation
- group health and life insurance
- product liability coverage if you make or sell a product; workmanship liability for services
- business use of vehicle coverage

Overall Home Attendant Site Evaluation

After you have gathered as much information as seems practical you may wish to evaluate several different locations. Here's a handy checklist. Using the "0" to "10" scale, grade these vital factors:

Factors to Consider

Factor	Grades 0-10
1. Customer convenience	_____
2. Availability of merchandise or raw materials	_____
3. Nearby competition	_____
4. Transportation availability and rates	_____
5. Quality and quantity of employees available	_____
6. Availability of parking facilities	_____

7. Adequacy of utilities (sewer, water, power, gas)   _____

8. Traffic flow   _____

9. Tax burden   _____

10. Quality of police and fire services   _____

11. Environmental factors   _____

12. Physical suitability for future expansion   _____

13. Provision for future expansion   _____

14. Vendor delivery access   _____

15. Personal convenience   _____

16. Cost of operation   _____

17. Other factors including how big you get without moving   _____

TOTALS   _____

Writing the Business Plan

Now that your research and plan development is nearing completion, it is time to move into action. If you are still in favor of going ahead, it is time to take several specific steps. The key one is to organize your dream scheme into a business plan.

What is it?

- As a business plan it is written by the Home Attendant Business owner with outside help as needed
- It is accurate and concise as a result of careful study
- It explains how the business will function in the marketplace
- It clearly depicts its operational characteristics
- It details how it will be financed
- It outlines how it will be managed
- It is the management and financial "blueprint" for start-up and profitable operation
- It serves as a prospectus for potential investors and lenders

Why create it?

- The process of putting the business plan together, including the thought that you put in before writing it, forces you to take an objective, critical, unemotional look at your entire business proposal
- The finished written plan is an operational tool which, when properly used, will help you manage your business and work toward its success
- The completed business plan is a means for communicating your ideas to others and provides the basis for financing your business

Who should write it?

- The Home Attendant owner to the extend possible
- Seek assistance in weak areas, such as:
    — accounting
    — insurance
    — capital requirements
    — operational forecasting
    — tax and legal requirements

When should a business plan be used?

- To make crucial start-up decisions
- To reassure lenders or backers
- To measure operations progress
- To test planning assumptions
- As a basis for adjusting forecasts
- To anticipate ongoing capital and cash requirements
- As the benchmark for good operations management

Proposed Outline for Home Attendant Business Plan

This outline is suggested for a small proprietorship or family business. Shape it to fit *your* unique needs. For more complex manufacturing or franchise operations see the Resource section for other options.

Part I - Business Organization

Cover page:

    A.   Business name:

           Street address:

           Mailing address:

           Telephone number:

           Owner(s) name(s):

Inside pages:

    B.   Business form:

           (proprietorship, partnership, corporation)

           If incorporated (state incorporation)

           Include copies of key subsidiary documents in an appendix.

Remember even partnerships require written agreements of terms and conditions to avoid later conflicts and to establish legal entities and equities. Corporations require charters, articles of incorporation and bylaws.

Part II - Business Purpose and Function

In this section, write an accurate yet, concise description of the business. Describe the business you plan to start in narrative form.

What is the principal activity? Be specific. Give product or service description(s):

- retail sales?

- manufacturing?

- service?

- other?

How will it be started?

- a new start up

- the expansion of an existing business

- purchase of a going business

- a franchise operation

- actual or projected start up date

Why will it succeed? Promote your idea!

- how and why this business will be successful

- what is unique about your business

- what is its market "niche"

What is your experience in this business? If you have a current resume of your career, include it in an appendix and reference it here. Otherwise write a narrative here and include a resume in the finished product. If you lack specific experience, detail how you plan to gain it, such as training, apprenticeship or working with partners who have experience.

The Marketing Plan

The marketing plan is the core of your business rationale. To develop a consistent sales growth an Home Attendant Business person much become knowledgeable about the market. To demonstrate your understanding, this section of the Home Attendant Business plan should seek to concisely answer several basic questions:

Who is your market?

- Describe the profile of your typical customer

  Age?

  Male, female, both?

  How many in family?

  Annual family income?

  Location?

  Buying patterns?

  Reason to buy from you?

Other?

- Biographically describe your trading area (i.e., county, state, national)

- Economically describe your trading area: (single family, average earnings, number of children)

How large is the market?

- Total units or dollars?

- Growing _____ Steadily _____ Decreasing _____

- If growing, annual growth rate. _____

Who is your competition?

No small business operates in a vacuum. Get to know and respect the competition. Target your marketing plans. Identify direct competitors (both in terms of geography and product lines), and those who are similar or marginally comparative. Begin by listing names, addresses and products or service. Detail briefly but concisely the following information concerning each of your competitors:

- Who are the nearest ones?

- How are their businesses similar or competitive to yours?

- Do you have a unique "niche"? Describe it.

- How will your service or product be better or more saleable than your competitors?

- Are their businesses growing? Stable? Declining? Why?

- What can be learned from observing their operations or talking to their present or former clients?

- Will you have competitive advantages or disadvantages? Be honest!

What percent of the market will you penetrate?
1. estimate the market in total units or dollars

2. estimate your planned volume

3. amount your volume will add to total market

4. subtract 3 from 2

Item 4 represents the amount of your planned volume that must be taken away from the competition.

What pricing and sales terms are you planning?

The primary consideration in pricing a product or service is the value that it represents to the customer. If, on the previous checklist of features, your product is truly ahead of the field, you can command a premium price. On the other hand, if it is a "me too" product, you may have to "buy" a share of the market to get your foothold and then try to move price up later. This is always risky and difficult. One rule will always hold: ultimately, the market will set the price. If your selling price does not exceed your costs and expenses by the margin necessary to keep your business healthy, you will fail. Know your competitors pricing policies. Send a friend to comparison shop. Is there discounting? Special sales? Price leaders? Make some "blind" phone calls. Detail your pricing policy.

What is your sales plan?

Describe how you will sell, distribute or service what you sell. Be specific. Below are outlined some common practices:

Direct Sales - by telephone or in person. The tremendous growth of individual sales representatives who sell by party bookings, door to door, and through distribution of call back promotional campaigns suggests that careful research is required to be profitable.

Mail Order - Specialized markets for leisure time or unique products have grown as more two income families find less time to shop. Be aware of recent mail order legislation and regulation.

Franchising -

a. You may decide to either buy into someone else's franchise as a franchisee, or

b. Create your own franchise operation that sells rights to specific territories or product lines to others. Each will require further legal, financial and marketing research.

Management Plan

Who will do what?

Be sure to include four basic sets of information:

1. State a personal history of principals and related work, hobby or volunteer experience (include formal resumes in Appendix)

2. List and describe specific duties and responsibilities of each

3. List benefits and other forms of compensation for each

46

4. Identify other professional resources available to the business: Example: Accountant, lawyer, insurance broker, banker. Describe relationship of each to business: Example "Accountant available on part-time hourly basis, as needed, initial agreement calls for services not to exceed x hours per month at $xx.xx per hour."

To make this section graphically clear, start with a simple organizational chart that lists specific tasks and shows, *who* (type of person is more important than an individual name other than for principals) will do *what* indicate by arrows, work flow and lines of responsibility and/or communications. Consider the following examples:

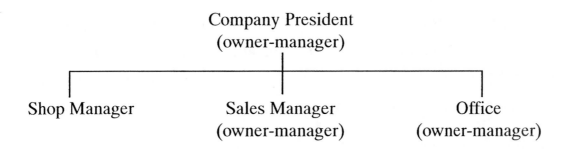

or like this?

As the service business grows, its organization chart could look like this:

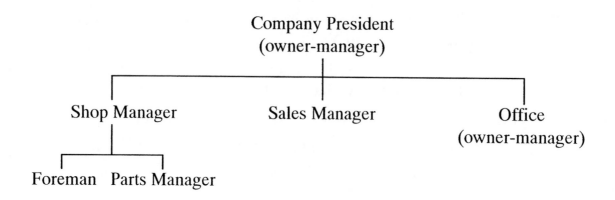

The Financial Plan

Clearly the most critical section of your business plan document is the financial plan. In formulating this part of the planning document, you will establish vital schedules that will guide the financial health of your business through the troubled waters of the first year and beyond.

Before going into the details of building the financial plan, it is important to realize that some basic knowledge of accounting is essential to the productive management of your business. If you are like most business owners, you probably have a deep and abiding interest in the product or services that you sell or intend to sell. You like to do what you do, and it is even more fulfilling that you are making money doing it. There is nothing wrong with that. Your conviction that what you are doing or making is worthwhile is vitally important to success. Nonetheless, the income of a coach who takes the greatest pride in producing a winning team will largely depend on someone keeping score of the wins and losses.

The business owner is no different. Your product or service may improve the condition of mankind for generations to come, but, unless you have access to an unlimited bankroll, you will fail if you don't make a profit. If you don't know what's going on in your business, you are not in a very good position to assure its profitability.

Most Home Attendant businesses will use the "cash" method of accounting with a system of record keeping that may be little more than a carefully annotated checkbook in which is recorded all receipts and all expenditures, backed up by a few forms of original entry (invoices, receipts, cash tickets). For a Sole Partnership, the business form assumed by this Management Aid, the very minimum of recorded information is that required to accurately complete the Federal Internal Revenue Service Form 1040, Schedule C. Other business types (partnerships, joint ventures, corporations) have similar requirements but use different tax forms.

If your business is, or will be, larger than just a small supplement to family income, you will need something more sophisticated. Stationery stores can provide you with several packaged small business account systems complete with simple journals and ledgers and detailed instructions in understandable language.

Should you feel that your accounting knowledge is so rudimentary that you will need professional assistance to establish your accounting system, the classified section of your telephone directory can lead you to a number of small business services that offer a complete range of accounting services. You can buy as much as you need, from a simple "pegboard" system all the way to computerized accounting, tax return service and monthly profitability consultation. Rates are reasonable for the services rendered and an investigative consultation will usually be free. Look under the heading, "Business Consultants," and make some calls.

Let's start by looking at the makeup of the financial plan for the business.

The Financial plan includes the following:

1. Financial Planning Assumptions - these are short statements of the conditions under which you plan to operate.

- Market health
- Date of start-up
- Sales build-up ($)
- Gross profit margin
- Equipment, furniture and fixtures required
- Payroll and other key expenses that will impact the financial plan

2. Operations Plan - Profit and Loss Projection - this is prepared for the first year's Budget. Appendix A-11.

3. Source of Funds Schedule - this shows the source(s) of your funds to capitalize the business and how they will be distributed among your fixed assets and working capital.

4. Pro Forma Balance Sheet - "Pro forma" refers to the fact that the balance sheet is before the fact, not actual. This form displays Assets, Liabilities and Equity of the business. This will indicate how much Investment will be required by the business and how much of it will be used as Working Capital in its operation.

5. Cash Flow Projection - this will forecast the flow of cash into and out of your business through the year. It helps you plan for staged purchasing, high volume months and slow periods.

Creating the Profit and Loss Projection.

Appendix A-11. Create a wide sheet of analysis paper with a three inch wide column at the extreme left and thirteen narrow columns across the page. Write at the top of the first page the planned name of your business. On the second line of the heading, write "Profit and Loss Projection." On the third line, write "First Year."

Then, note the headings on Appendix A-11 and copy them onto your 12-column sheet, copy the headings from the similar area on Exhibit A. Then follow the example set by Appendix A-11 and list all of the other components of your income, cost and expense structure. You may add or delete specific loans of expense to suit your business plan. Guard against consolidating too many types of expenses under one account lest you lose control of the components. At the same time, don't try to break down expenses so discretely that accounting becomes a nuisance instead of a management tool. Once again, Exhibit A provides ample detail for most businesses.

Now, in the small column just to the left of the first monthly column, you will want to note which of the items in the left-hand column are to be estimated on a monthly (M) or yearly (Y) basis. Items such as Sales, Cost of Sales and Variable expenses will be estimated monthly based on planned volume and seasonal or other estimated fluctuations. Fixed Expenses can usually be estimated on a yearly basis and divided by twelve to arrive at even monthly values. The "M" and "Y" designations will be used later to distinguish between variable and fixed expense.

Depreciation allowances for Fixed Assets such as production equipment, office furniture and machines, vehicles, etc. will be calculated from the Source of Funds Schedule.

Appendix A-11 describes line by line how the values on the Profit and Loss Projection are developed. Use this as your guide.

Source of Funds Schedule

To create this schedule, you will need to create a list of all the Assets that you intend to use in your business, how much investment each will require and the source of funds to capitalize them. A sample of such a list is shown below:

Asset	Cost	Source of Funds
Cash	$2,500	Personal savings
Accounts Receivable	3,000	From profits
Inventory	2,000	Vendor credit
Pickup truck	5,000	Currently owned
Packaging machine	10,000	Installment purchase
Office desk and chair	300	Currently owned
Calculator	75	Personal cash
Electric typewriter*	500	Personal savings

* A note about office equipment, test use or rent two or more brands that appear to meet your needs and select the one with which you feel most comfortable. Don't be afraid to ask others who have had to make this decision for advice. Compatibility of your system with those of potential typesetting services or printers should be of high considerations. If you are not quite sure, consider renting or leasing the equipment until you are. Service contracts on such complex electronic gear are usually a good insurance policy.

Before you leave your Source of Funds Schedule, indicate the number of months (years x 12) of useful life for depreciable fixed assets. (An example, the pickup truck, the packaging machine and the furniture and office equipment would be depreciable.) Generally, any individual item of equipment, furniture, fixtures, vehicles, etc., costing over $100 should be depreciated. For more information on allowances for depreciation, you can get free publications and assistance from your local Internal Revenue Service office. Divided the cost of each fixed asset item by the number or months over which it will be depreciated. You will need this data to enter as monthly depreciation on your Profit and Loss Projection. All of the data on the Source of Funds Schedule will be needed to create the Balance Sheet.

Creating the Pro Forma Balance Sheet

Appendix A-13. This is the Balance Sheet Form. There are a number of variations of this form and you may find it prudent to ask your banker for the form that the bank uses for small business. It will make it easier for them to evaluate the health of your business. Use this to get started and transfer the data to your preferred form later. Accompanying Appendix A-12 which describes line by line how to develop the Balance Sheet.

Even though you may plan to stage the purchase of some assets through the year, for the purpose of this pro forma Balance Sheet, assume that all assets will be provided at the start-up.

Cash Flow Projection

An important subsidiary schedule to your financial plan is a monthly Cash Flow Projection. Prudent business management practice is to keep no more cash in the business than is needed to operate it and to protect it from catastrophe. In most small businesses, the problem is rarely one of having too much cash. A Cash Flow Projection is made to advise management of the amount of cash that is going to be absorbed by the operation of the business and compares it against the amount that will be available.

SBA has created an excellent form for this purpose and it is shown as Appendix B. Your projection should be prepared on 13-column analysis paper to allow for a twelve-month projection. Appendix B represents a line by line description and explanation of the components of the Cash Flow Projection which provides a step-by-step method of preparation.

Resources

U.S. Small Business Administration
Office of Business Development

Business Development Publication
MP15

Home Attendant
Business Associations for the Entrepreneur

American Licensed Practical Nurse Assoc. (ALPNA)
1090 Vermont Ave. NW, Ste. 1200
Washington, DC 20005
Paul M. Tendler, Exec. Dir.
PH: (202) 682-5800   FX: (202) 682-0168
Founded: 1984   Members: 6,200

American Nursing Care Foundation (ANCF)
P.O. Box 104
Ottawa, KS 66067-0104
Steve P. Grosline, Exec. Dir.
Founded: 1982   Members: 210

Hospice Nursing Assoc. (HNA)
5512 N. Umberland St.
Pittsburgh, PA 15217-1131
Madalon Amanta, Exec. Dir.
PH: (412) 687-3231   FX: (412) 687-9095
Founded: 1985   Members: 1,200

National Alliance of Nurse Practitioners (NANP)
325 Pennsylvania Ave. SE
Washington, DC 20003-1100
Norma Small, Chairperson
PH: (202) 675-6350
Founded: 1985   Members: 30,000

Notes _____

Chapter 7

Managing The Business

Delegating work, responsibility, and authority is difficult in a small business because it means letting others make decisions which involved spending the owner/manager's money. At a minimum, he should delegate enough authority to get the work done, to allow assistants to take initiative, and to keep the operation moving in his absence. Coaching those who carry responsibility and authority in self-improvement is essential and emphasis in allowing competent assistants to perform in their own style rather than insisting that things be done exactly as the owner/manager would personally do them is important. "Let others take care of the details" is the meaning of delegating work and responsibility. In theory, the same principles for getting work done through other people apply whether you have 25 employees and one top assistant or 150 to 200 employees and several keymen yet, putting the principles into practice is often difficult.

Delegation is perhaps the hardest job owner/managers have to learn. Some never do. They insist on handling many details and work themselves into early graves. Others pay lip service to the idea but actually run a one-man shop. They give their assistants many responsibilities but little or no authority. Authority is the fuel that makes the machine go when you delegate word and responsibility. If an owner/manager is to run a successful company, he must delegate authority properly. How much authority is proper depends on your situation. At a minimum, you should delegate enough authority: (1) to get the work done, (2) to allow keymen to take initiative, (3) to keep things going in your absence.

The person who fills a key management spot in the organization must either be a manager or be capable of becoming one. A manager's chief job is to plan, direct, and coordinate the work of others. He should possess the three "I's" — Initiative, Interest, and Imagination. The manager of a department must have enough self-drive to start and keep things moving. Personality traits must be considered. A keyman should be strong-willed enough to overcome opposition when necessary.

When you manage through others, it is essential that you keep control. You do it by holding a subordinate responsible for his actions and checking the results of those actions. In controlling your assistants, try to strike a balance. You should not get into a keyman's operations so closely that you are "in his hair" nor should you be so far removed that you lose control of things.

You need feedback to keep yourself informed. Reports provide a way to get the right kind of feedback at the right time. This can be daily, weekly, or monthly depending on how soon you need the information. Each department head can report his progress, or lack of it, in the unit of production that is appropriate for his activity; for example, items packed in the shipping room, sales per territory, hours of work per employee.

For the owner/manager, delegation does not end with good control. It involves coaching as well, because management ability is not required automatically. You have to teach it. Just as important, you have to keep your managers informed just as you would be if you were doing their jobs.

Part of your job is to see that they get the facts they need for making their decisions. You should be certain that you convey your thinking when you coach your assistants. Sometimes words can be inconsistent with thoughts. Ask questions to make sure that the listener understands your meaning. In other words, delegation can only be effective when you have good communications.

Sometimes an owner/manager finds himself involved in many operational details even though he does everything that is necessary for delegation of responsibility. In spite of defining authority, delegation, keeping control, and coaching, he is still burdened with detailed work. Usually, he had failed to do one vital thing. He has refused to stand back and let the wheels turn.

If the owner/manager is to make delegation work, he must allow his subordinates freedom to do things their way. He and the company are in trouble if he tries to measure his assistants by whether they do a particular task exactly as he would do it. They should be judged by their results — not their methods. No two persons react exactly the same in every situation. Be prepared to see some action taken differently from the way in which you would do it even though your policies are well defined. Of course, if an assistant strays too far from policy, you need to bring him back in line. You cannot afford second-guessing.

You should also keep in mind that when an owner/manager second-guesses his assistants, he risks destroying their self-confidence. If the assistant does not run his department to your satisfaction and if his shortcomings cannot be overcome, then replace him. But when results prove his effectiveness, it is good practice to avoid picking at each move he makes.

Notes _____

Chapter 8

Business Resource Information

oks

The Big Idea: How Business Innovators Get Great Ideas to Market,
    by Steven D. Strauss (Dearborn, 2001).

Blue's Clues for Success: The 8 Secrets Behind a Phenomenal Business,
    by Diane Tracy (Dearborn, 2001).

The E-Myth Revised: Why Most Small Businesses Don't Work and What to Do About It,
    by Micheal E. Gerber (Harper Business, 1995).

Guerrilla Marketing: Secrets for Making Big Profits from Your Small Business,
    by Jay Conrad Levinson (Mariner Books, 1998).

Own Your Own Corporation: Why the Rich Own Their Own Companies and Everyone Else Works for them,
    by Garrett Sutton, Robert T. Kiyosaki, and Ann Blackman (Warner Books, 2001).

Portratis of Success: 9 Keys to Sustaining Value in Any Business,
    by James Olan Hutcheson (Dearborn, 2002).

Small Time Operator: How to Start Your Own Business, Keep Your Books, Pay Your Taxes, and Stay Out of Trouble, (Small Time Operator, 25th Edition)
    by Bernard B. Kamoroff, (Bell Springs Publishing, 2000).

Successful Business Planning in 30 Days: A Step-by-Step Guide for Writing a Business Plan and Starting Your Own Business,
    by Peter J. Patsula (Patsul Media, 2000).

What No One Ever Tells You About Starting Your Own Business: Real Life Start-Up Advice from 101 Successful Entrepreneurs,
    by Jan Norman (Upstart Publishing, 1999).

Associations and Organizations

U.S. Department of Commerce
14th Street and Constitution Avenue NW
Room 5055
Washington, DC 20210
Phone: 202-482-5061
Web site: *rvwm.mbda.gov*

U.S. Department of Labor
200 Constitution Avenue NW
Washington, DC 20210
Web site: *www.dol.gov*

Federal Trade Commission
600 Pennsylvania Avenue NW
Washington, DC 20580
General information: 202-326-2222
Anti-trust and competition issues: 202-326-3300
Web site: *www.ftc.gov*

U.S. Small Business Administration (SBA)
403 3rd Street SW
Washington, DC 20416
Phone: 202-205-7701
Web site: *www.sba.gov*

SBA Regional Offices
- Region 1, Boston: 617-565-8415
- Region 2, New York: 212-264-1450
- Region 3, King of Prussia, PA: 215-962-3700
- Region 4, Atlanta: 404-347-995
- Region 5, Chicago: 310-353-5000
- Region 6, Ft. Worth, TX: 817-885-6581
- Region 7, Kansas City, MO: 816-374-6380
- Region 8, Denver: 303-844-0500
- Region 9, San Francisco: 415-744-2118
- Region 10, Seattle: 206-553-7310

Internal Revenue Service
Washington, DC 20224
Phone: 800429-1040
Web site: *www.irs.ustres.gov*

The IRS has an expansive Web site where you can find a great deal of tax help and a state-by-state guide for locating state tax information. There are also numerous tax publications (all numbered) including:

- Tax Guide for Small Business, Publication #334
- Self-Employment Tax, Publication #533
- Business Expenses, Publication #535

For tax forms go to *www.irs.ustres.gov/forms*

International Franchise Association
1350 New York Avenue NW
Suite 900
Washington, DC 20005-4709
Phone: 202-628-8000

American Association of Franchises and Dealers
P.O. Box 81887
San Diego, CA 92138-1887
Phone: 800-733-9858
Web site: *www.aafd.org*

Associations and Organizations

tional Association of Women
Business Owners
11 K Street NW
ite 1300
ashington, DC 20005
one: 202-347-8686
x: 202-347-4130
formation service line: 800-556-2926
eb site: *www.nawbo.org*

e National Association for the Self-Employed
23 15 Street NW
ite 1200
ashington, DC 20005-2600
one: 202-466-2100
eb site: *www.nase.com*
e NASE works to help the self-employed
ake their businesses successful and provides
merous benefits and services. It was formed
er twenty years ago by small business owners.

ccupational Safety and Health Administra-
n (OSHA)
0 Constitution Avenue NW
ashington, DC 20210
eb site: *www.osha-slc.gov*

stitute For Occupational Safety and Health
one: 800-35-NIOSH or 513-533-8328
eb site: *www.cdc.gov/niosh*

n & Bradstreet
stin, Texas 78731
one: 800-234-3867
eb site: *www.dnb.com*
r over 160 years, D&B has been providing
mpanies with information and assistance in
king key business decisions.

American Entrepreneurs for
  Economic Growth
1655 North Fort Myer Drive
Suite 850
Arlington, VA 22209
Phone: 703-524-3743
Web site: *www.aeeg.org*

National Association of
  Home-Based Businesses
10451 Mill Run Circle
Suite 400
Owings Mills, MD 21117
Phone: 410-363-3698
Web site: *www.usahomebusiness.com*

U.S. Census Bureau
Washington DC 20233
Phone: 301-457-4608
Web site: *www.census.gov*

U.S. Patent and Trademark Office
General Information Services Division
Crystal Plaza 3, Room 2CO2
Washington, DC 20231
Phone: 800-786-9199 or 703-308-4357
Web site: *www.uspto.gov*

U.S. Securities & Exchange Commission
450 Fifth Street NW
Washington, DC 20549
Office of Investor Education
  and Assistance: 202-942-7040
Web site: *www.sec.gov*

Associations and Organizations

**American Association of
  Home Based Businesses**
Fax: 301-963-7042
P.O. Box 10023
Rockville, MD 20849
Website: *www.aahbb.org*

American Small Businesses Association
800-942-2722
8773 IL Route 75E
Rock City, IL 61070

Home Business Institute
561-865-0865
P.O. Box 480215
Delray Beach, FL 33448
Website: *www.hbiweb.com*

Marketing Research Association
860-257-4008
1344 Silas Deane Highway, Suite 306,
Rocky Hill, CT 06067
Website: *www.mra-net.org*

**National Association of the
  Self-Employed (NASE)**
800-252-NASE (800-232-6273)
P.O. Box 612067
DFW Airport
Dallas, TX 75261-2067
Website: *www.nase.org*

Magazines

Entrepreneur Magazine, Business Start-Ups Magazine, and **Entrepreneur's Home Office Entrepreneur Media, Inc.**
92 Morse Avenue
Irvine, CA 92614
Phone: 714-261-2325
Web site: *www.entrepreneurmag.com*

Forbes
Fifth Avenue
New York, NY 10011
Phone: 212-620-2200
Web site: *www.forbes.com*

Inc. Magazine
Commercial Wharf
Boston, MA 02110
Phone: 617-248-8000 or 800-2340999
Web site: *www.inc.com*

My Business Magazine
Hammock Publishing, Inc.
22 West End Avenue
Suite 700
Nashville, TN 37203
Phone: 615-385-9745

Consumer Goods Manufacturer
Edgell Communications
10 West Hanover Avenue
Suite 107
Randolph, NJ 07869

Minority Business Entrepreneur
3528 Torrance Boulevard
Suite 101
Torrance, CA 90503
Phone: 310-540-9398
Web site: *www.mbemag.com*

Workforce ACC Communications
245 Fischer Avenue
Suite B-2
Costa Mesa, CA 92626
Phone: 714-751-4106
Web site: *www.workforceonline.com*

Websites

www.allbusiness.com
A comprehensive site with resources for small and medium sized businesses.

www.bizweb.com
A guide to some 47,000 companies.

www.bplan.com
Numerous sample business plans for various industries.

www.bspage.com
The Business Start page includes a short course on starting a business, tips, and reviews of top business books.

www.business.gov
The U.S. Business Advisor is a one-stop shop for working with the many government agencies that impact upon business.

www.businessfinance. com
A major online source for finding potential investors.

www.businessnation.com
Business news, a library, discussions, opportunities, and resources.

www.businesstown.com
Information and articles from starting to selling your business.

www.catalogconsultancy.com
Information and guidance for catalog and direct mail businesses.

www.chamber-of-commerce.com
Links to local chamber of commerce Web sites, and e-mail addresses.

www.financenet.com
Sponsored by the US Chief Financial Officers Council, FinanceNet has a wealth of information and resources available specializing in public financial management.

www.globalbizdirectory.com
Massive director of retail, agricultural, mining, and numerous other business-related organizations and associations. Includes a state-by-state and international listing database.

www.gomez.com
Gomez offers business new and detailed report cards and consumer responses on e-commerce Web sites in various sectors.

www.homebusiness.com
Detailed information and business solutions for the home base business.

www.hoovers.com
Provides detailed business and company information, industry report links, professional help, business news, and more.

www.ideacafe.com
A good place for news, tips, expert advice ideas, and schmoozing with other small business owners.

www.inc.com
A wealth of articles and advice about starting and growing your business from the folks at Inc. Magazine.

www.marketingsource.com/associations
Find any association in any industry at this valuable resource site.

www.morebusiness.com
Articles, tips, sample business and marketing plans, legal forms contracts, a newsletter, and more offered for entrepreneurs.

www.nasbic.org
The National Association of Small Business Investment Companies promotes growth in the business sector through numerous programs.

Notes _____

A Concise Guide To Starting Your Own Business

Guide Overview

A concise overview of the complete guide to starting and operating a successful business.

The following topics are presented:

- Business Plan for Small Businesses.
- Getting Started
- Deciding Where To Start The Business
- Business Patronage Statistics
- Site Location
- Site Selection Criteria — Some General Questions.
- Choosing The Proper Method of Organization
- What Is A Corporation?
- Estimating Start-up Costs
- Preparing An Income Statement
- Preparing A Balance Sheet
- Marketing The Business
- Marketing Planning — An Outline for Marketing
- Advertising Media
- Management and Getting The Work Done
- Sample Organization Chart
- Summary of the Business Plan
- Guide Summary
- Reference Materials

Business Plan for Small Businesses

I.   Type of Business

II.   Location

III.   Target Market

IV.   Planning Process

V.   Organizational Structure

VI.   Staffing Procedures

VII.   Control

VIII.   Market Strategy

IX.   Financial Planning

X.   Budgeted Balance Sheet

XI.   Budgeted Income Statement

XII.   Budgeted Cash Flow Statement

XIII.   Break-even Chart

Getting Started

Following is a list of what you need to accomplish to insure that your business endeavor will head in the right direction.

1. Define your educational background and work experience

2. Survey all basic types of businesses.

3. Define what type of business matches your experience and educational background.

4. Choose only the business that you would like to own and operate.

5. Define what products or services your business will be marketing.

6. Define who will be using your products/services.

7. Define why they will be purchasing your products/services.

8. List all competitors in your marketing area.

Deciding Where to Start the Business

Will your business fulfill a need in the area you plan to bring your business to? This section provides you with some important information you need to examine before taking your ideas any further:

1. Decide where you want to live.

2. Choose several areas that would match your priorities.

3. Use the list that follows as a guide to see if your location will match the estimated population needed to support your business. The numbers which follow the type of business indicate the typical number of inhabitants per year.

Business Patronage Statistics

Food Stores
Grocery Stores 1,534
Meat and Fish
(Sea Food) Markets . . . 17,876
Candy, Nut, and
Confectionery Stores . . 31,409
Retail Bakeries 12,563
Dairy Products Stores . . . 41,587

Eating and Drinking
Restaurant, Lunch Rooms . 1,583
Cafeterias 19,341
Refreshment Places 3,622
Drinking Places 2,414

General Merchandise
Variety Stores 10,373
General Merchandise 9,837

Apparel/Accessories Stores
Women's Ready-To-
Wear Stores 7,102
Women's Accessory and
Specialty Stores 25,824
Men's and Boy's Clothing
and Furnishings 11,832
Family Clothing 16,890
Shoe Stores 9,350

Furniture, Home Furnishings, and Equipment Stores
Furniture Stores 7,210
Floor Covering 29,543
Drapery, Curtains, and
Upholstery Stores 62,585
House, Appliances 12,485
Radios and TV's 20,346
Record Shops 112,144
Musical Instruments 46,332

Building Materials, Hardware, and Farm Equipment Dealers
Lumber and other Building
Materials Dealers 8,124
Paint, Glass, and Wallpaper
Stores 22,454
Hardware Stores 10,206
Farm Equipment Dealers . 14,793

Automotive Dealers
Motor Vehicle Dealers,
New and Used Cars 6,000
Motor Vehicle Dealers,
Used Cars only 17,160
Tire, battery, and
Accessory Dealers 8,800

Boat Dealers 61,500

Household Trailer Dealers . 44,746

Gasoline Service Stations . . . 1,395

Miscellaneous
Antique and Secondhand
Stores 17,170
Book and Stationery Stores 28,580
Drugstores 4,268
Florists 13,531
Fuel Oil Dealers 25,000
Garden Supply Stores . . . 65,000
Gift, Novelty Shops 26,000
Hobby, Toy, and Game
Shops 61,000
Jewelry Stores 13,400
Optical Goods Stores 62,800
Sporting Goods Store 27,000

From *Starting and Managing a Small Business of Your Own, 1973;*
Small Business Administration, Washington, DC

Page A-6

Site Location

1. Define your number of inhabitants per store.

2. Locate several sites/locations that will match your inhabitants per stores.

3. Define population and its growth potential.

4. Define local ordinances and zoning regulations that you will need in order to start your type of business.

5. Define your trading area and all competitors in your trading area.

6. Define parking need, for your kind of business.

7. Define special needs, etc., lighting, heating, ventilation.

8. Define rental cost of site/location.

9. Define why customers will come to your site/location.

10. Define the future of your site/location as to population growth.

11. Define your space needs and match with site/location selection.

12. Define the image of your business and make sure it matches your site/location.

Site Selection Criteria — Some General Questions

- Is the site centrally located to reach my market?

- What is the transportation availability and what are the rates?

- What provisions for future expansion can I make:

- What is the topography of the site (slope and foundation)?

- What is the housing availability for workers and managers?

- What environmental factors (schools, cultural, community atmosphere) might affect my business and my employees?

- What will the quality of this site be in 5 years, 10 years, 25 years?

- What is my estimate of this site in relation to my major competitor?

- What other media are available for advertising? How many radio and television stations are there?

- Is the Quantity and quality of available labor concentrated in a given area in the city or town? If so, is commuting a way of living in that city or town?

- Is the city centrally located to my suppliers?

- What are the labor conditions, including such things as relationships with the business community and average wages and salaries paid?

- Is the local business climate healthy, or are business failures especially high in the area?

- What about tax requirements? Is there a city business tax? Income tax? What is the property tax rate? Is there a personal property tax? Are there other special taxes?

- Is the available police and fire protection adequate?

- Is the city or town basically well planned and managed in terms of such items as electric power, sewage, and paved streets and sidewalks?

Choosing the Proper Method of Organization

Listed below are legal forms of business available to the small business entrepreneur:

Sole Proprietorship

Advantages
- Simple to start
- All profits to owner
- Owner in direct control
- Easy entry and exit
- Taxed as individual

Disadvantages
- Unlimited liability
- "Jack-of-all-trades"
- Capital requirement limited
- Limited life
- Employee turn-over

Partnership

Advantages
- Easy to originate
- Credit rating
- Talent combination
- Legal Contract

Disadvantages
- Unlimited liability
- Misunderstandings
- Partner withdrawal
- Regulations

Corporation

Advantages
- Limited liability
- Expansion potential
- Transfer of ownership
- Retain employees

Disadvantages
- Double taxation
- Charter restrictions
- Employee motivation
- Legal regulations

What Is A Corporation?

A corporation is an artificial being, invisible, intangible, and existing only in contemplation of the law," wrote Chief Justice John Marshall. In other words, the corporation exists as a separate entity apart from its owners, the shareholders. It makes contracts; it is liable; it pays taxes. It is a "legal person".

The corporation is the most complex of the three major forms of business ownership. The corporation stands as a separate legal entity in the eyes of the law. The life of the corporation is independent of the owners' lives. Because the owners, called shareholders, are legally separate from the corporation, they can sell their interests in the business without affecting the continuation of the business. When a corporation is founded, it accepts the regulations and restrictions placed on it by the state in which it is incorporated and any other state in which it chooses to do business. Generally, the corporation must report its financial operations to the state's attorney general on an annual basis.

Page A-10

Estimating Start-up Costs

Item	Amount
Fixtures and Equipment	$ _____
Building & Land (If Needed)	_____
Store and/or Office Supplies	_____
Remodeling and Decorating	_____
Deposits on Utilities	_____
Insurance	_____
Installation of Fixtures	_____
Legal Fees	_____
Professional Fees	_____
Telephone	_____
Rental	_____
Salaries and Wages	_____
Inventory if Retailing	_____
Licenses and Permits	_____
Advertising and Promotion	_____
TOTAL Estimated Start-up Cost	$ _____

Preparing An Income Statement

What is an Income Statement?

The income statement shows the income received and the expenses incurred over a period of time. Income received (sales) comes essentially from the sales of the merchandise or service which your business is formed to sell. Expenses incurred are the expired costs that have been incurred during the same period of time.

Plan A Budgeted Income Statement For One Year

1. Project Total Sales
2. Estimate Total Expenditures
3. Example Listed Below for Income Statement

Percents	1	2	3	4	5	6	7	8	9	10	11	12
Sales												
Cost of Sales												
Gross Profit												
Expenditure												
Rent Expense												
Supplies												
Wages/Salaries												
Utilities												
Insurance												
Depreciation												
Interest												
Miscellaneous												
Net Profit												

Preparing A Balance Sheet

What is a Balance Sheet?

The balance sheet shows the assets, liabilities and owner's net worth in a business as of a given date.

- Assets are the things owned by your business, including both physical things and claims against others.
- Liabilities are the amounts owned to others, the creditors of the firm.
- Net worth or owner's equity is the owner's claim to the assets after liabilities are accounted for.

A Budgeted Balance Sheet For One Year

- List all your business property at their cost to you: these are your assets.
- List all debts, or what your business owes on all your property; these are your liabilities.
- Take your total property balance (Assets), and subtract the total amount you owe (Liabilities).
- The balance is what you own in your business called (Owner's equity).
- Add Total Liabilities (2) & Total Owner's Equity (3).
- Listed on the next page is an example of a balance sheet.

NAME OF BUSINESS
BALANCE SHEET
DATE

ASSETS
Current Assets
  Cash   _____
  Accounts Receivable   _____
Merchandise Inventories   _____
    TOTAL CURRENT ASSETS   _____

Fixed Assets
  Land   _____
  Building   _____
  Equipment   _____
    TOTAL FIXED ASSETS   _____
      TOTAL ASSETS   1). _____

LIABILITIES
Current Liabilities
  Accounts Payable   _____
  Note Payable   _____
  Payroll Taxes Payable   _____
    TOTAL CURRENT LIABILITIES   _____

Long-term Liabilities
  Mortgage Payable   _____
  Long-term Note   _____
    TOTAL LONG-TERM LIABILITIES   _____
      TOTAL LIABILITIES   2). _____

OWNER'S EQUITY
Proprietor's Capital   3). _____

    TOTAL LIABILITIES & OWNER'S EQUITY   (2 &3). _____

Page A-14

Marketing The Business

1. Define Your Market
   • Type of Customers
   • Age, Income, Occupation of your customers
   • Type of Trading Area

2. Promotion of Your Business
   • Advertising
   • Setting your Image

3. Customer Policy Plan
   • Develop a Customer Profile
   • Customer Services
   • Customer Needs

4. Pricing Your Products/Services
   • Know all your Costs
   • Know your Profit Margin
   • Know Competitor's Price
   • Know what Return you want on your Investment

5. Sales Promotion
   • Coupons
   • Contests
   • Displays
   • Demonstrations
   • Giveaways
   • Banners

6. Public Relations
   • Newspaper Article
   • Contact Trade Association
   • Radio Promotion
   • TV Promotion

7. Segmentation of your Market
   • Age
   • Occupation
   • Income
   • Location
   • Education
   • Hobbies

Marketing Planning

Outline for Marketing

I. Product/Service Concept:
  a. Name of product or service
  b. Descriptive characteristics of product or service
  c. Unit sales
  d. Analysis of market trends

II. Number of Customers in your Market Area:
  a. Profile of customers
  b. Average customer expenditure
  c. Total market

III. Your Market Potential:
  a. Total market divided by competition
  b. Total market multiplied by percent who will buy your product

IV. Needs of Customers:
  a. Identification
  b. Pleasure
  c. Social approval
  d. Personal interest
  e. Price

V. Direct Marketing Sources:
  a. Trade magazines
  b. Trade associations
  c. Small Business Administration (SBA)
  d. Government Publications
  e. Yellow pages
  f. Marketing directories

VI Customer Profile:
  a. Geographical
  b. Gender
  c. Age range
  d. Income brackets
  e. Occupation
  f. Educational level

Page A-16

Advertising Media

Medium	Market Coverage	Type of Audience
Daily newspaper	Single community or entire metro area: zoned editions sometimes available	General
Weekly newspaper	Single Community	Residents
Telephone Directory	Geographical area or occupational field served by the directory	Active shoppers for goods or services
Direct mail audience	Controlled by the advertiser	Controlled
Radio audience	Definable market area	Selected
Television audience	Definable market area surrounding TV Stations	Various
Outdoor	Entire metro area	General auto drivers
Magazine	Entire metro area or magazine region	Selected audience

Management and Getting the Work Done

1. Define your objective for starting your business.

2. Define your goals: profit growth for first three years.

3. Develop an organization chart of your business.

4. Define your personal needs.
   - Hiring proper employees
   - Training employees
   - Motivation

5. Define all responsibility for each person in your business.

6. Define all authority.
   - Who will hire and fire?
   - Who will select and train all personnel?
   - Who will keep the important records as to inventory, purchasing, sales records, cash records, etc.?

7. Define all laws and regulations that will be requirements for operating your business.

8. Review all duties and tasks with all your employees.

9. Write a summary of all the important tasks that you want to finish in your first year in business.

Sample Organization Chart

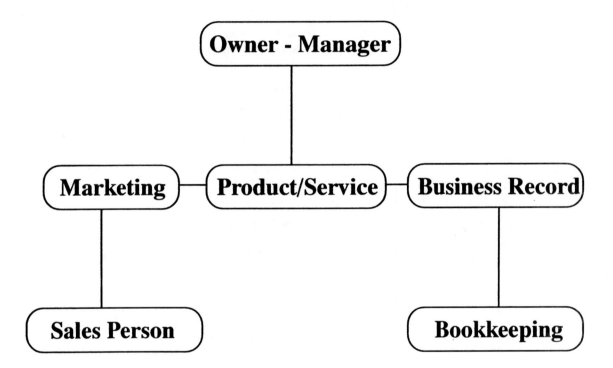

Summary of The Business Plan

Name of Business
BUSINESS PLAN
Date

1. Define your business
    *   Name all principals
    *   Address and phone number

2. Define your products or services

3. Define your market

4. Define your site or location

5. Advertising Plan
    *   Budget
    *   Media

6. Chart of Start-up cost

7. Worksheet of Income Statement
    *   Revenue/Income
    *   Expenses

8. Worksheet of Balance Sheet
    *   Assets (Property)
    *   Capital (Owner's Equity)
    *   Liabilities (Debts)

9. Personnel Outline
    *   Number of Employees
    *   Staffing & Training

10. Management Organization
    *   Organization Chart
    *   Evaluation Policy
    *   Job Profile

11. Special Statement
    *   3-Year Sales Schedule
    *   Cash Flow
    *   3-Year Expense Schedule

Appendix A Summary

1. Contact your State Commerce Department for guidelines in starting your business.

2. Contact your City/County Clerk for guidelines in starting your business.

3. Contact all other Governmental Centers that will furnish you all the legal regulations and tax laws that will effect your business.
   - State Government
   - Internal Revenue Service
   - State Employment Security Commission
   - Department of Treasury
   - City Governmental Units

     a. Fire
     b. Police
     c. Zoning
     d. Building Permits
     e. Health
     f. Water & Sewage

4. Township Government
   - Local Legal Requirements
   - Local Taxes
   - Local Health Permits
   - Local Zoning Laws

Reference Materials

Management Aids Titles

Contact the

**Small Business Administration
P.O. Box 15434
Fort Worth, TX 76119**

for the following booklets:

- Number 2.025   **Thinking About Going Into Business**
- Number 2.010   **Planning and Goal Setting For Business**
- Number 1.016   **Sound Cash Management**
- Number 1.001   **The A.B.C's. of Borrowing**
- Number 1.008   **Break-even Analysis**
- Number 2.022   **Business Plan For Service Firms**
- Number 2.023   **Business Plans for Retail Firms**

Notes

Appendix B

HOUSEHOLD NEEDS

Many small business start-ups fail due to their inability to support their owners. Rarely do new businesses support their owners from the start. However, many individuals fail to recognize this fact. In addition, then, to a sound business plan, it is necessary for an owner to project the household cash needs month-by-month for the first three years of the business' operation. As a new business owner, you should be able to support yourself until your new business is able to support you in a manner to which you are accustomed.

MONTHLY HOUSEHOLD CASH NEEDS

Regular NON-BUSINESS Income
Spouse's salary _____
Investment income _____
Social security _____
Other income _____
Retirement benefits _____
Less taxes _____
Net monthly income ===========

Regular Monthly Expenses

Housing
Mortgage/Rent _____
Utilities _____
Homeowner's insurance _____
Property taxes _____
Home repairs _____

Living Expenses
Groceries _____
Telephone _____
Tuition _____
Transportation _____
Meals _____
Child care _____
Medical expenses _____
Clothing _____
Personal _____

Insurance Premiums
Life insurance _____
Disability insurance _____
Auto insurance _____
Medical insurance _____

Debt Repayment
Auto loans _____
Consumer debt _____

Discretionary Expenses
Entertainment _____
Vacation _____
Gifts _____
Retirement contributions _____
Investment savings _____
Charitable contributions _____
Dues, magazines, etc. _____
Professional fees _____
Other _____

Total Monthly Expenses ===========

Monthly Surplus/Deficit ===========

Total Year Surplus/Deficit ===========
(Monthly x 12)

Available Assets to Cover Deficit
Checking accounts _____
Savings accounts _____
Money market accounts _____
Personal credit lines _____
Marketable securities _____
Lump-sum retirement/
    severance _____
Other assets _____

Total Assets ===========

NEEDED RESERVES
    Total Assets-Deficit ===========

PERSONAL FINANCIAL STATEMENT

This is a picture of your personal financial condition to date. It is a very important part of any loan application and/or interview, especially when a loan for a projected new business is under consideration.

PERSONAL FINANCIAL STATEMENT

_____   _____ , 19 _____

Assets
Cash
Savings accounts   _____
Stocks, bonds, other securities   _____
Accounts/Notes receivable   _____
Life insurance cash value   _____
Rebates/Refunds   _____
Autos/Other vehicles   _____
Real estate   _____
Vested pension plan/Retirement accounts   _____
Other assets   _____

                              TOTAL ASSETS $ _____

Liabilities

Accounts payable
Contracts payable   _____
Notes payable   _____
Taxes   _____
Real estate loans   _____
Other liabilities   _____

                          TOTAL LIABILITIES $ _____

TOTAL ASSETS $ _____

LESS TOTAL LIABILITIES $ _____

                              NET WORTH $ _____

BALANCE SHEET

A balance sheet is a current financial statement. It is a dollars and cents description of your business (existing or projected) which lists all of its assets and liabilities.

BALANCE SHEET

_____ _____ , 19 _____

	YEAR 1	YEAR II
Current Assets		
Cash	_____	_____
Accounts receivable	_____	_____
Inventory	_____	_____
Fixed Assets		
Real estate	_____	_____
Fixtures and equipment	_____	_____
Vehicles	_____	_____
Other Assets		
License	_____	_____
Goodwill	_____	_____
TOTAL ASSETS	$_____	$_____
Current Liabilities		
Notes payable (due within 1 year)	$_____	$_____
Accounts payable	_____	_____
Accrued expenses	_____	_____
Taxes owed	_____	_____
Long-Term Liabilities		
Notes payable (due after 1 year)	_____	_____
Other	_____	_____
TOTAL LIABILITIES	$_____	$_____
NETWORTH (ASSETS minus LIABILITIES)	$_____	$_____

TOTAL LIABILITIES plus NET WORTH should equal ASSETS

PROFIT AND LOSS STATEMENT

A profit and loss statement is a detailed earnings statement for the previous full year (if you are already in business). Existing businesses are also required to show a profit and loss statement for the current period to the date of the balance sheet.

PROJECTED PROFIT AND LOSS STATEMENT

	Month 1	Month 2	Month 3	Month 4	Month 5	Month 6	Month 7	Month 8	Month 9	Month 10	Month 11	Month 12
Total Net Sales												
Cost of Sales												
GROSS PROFIT												
Controllable Expenses												
Salaries												
Payroll taxes												
Security												
Advertising												
Automobile												
Dues and subscriptions												
Legal and accounting												
Office supplies												
Telephone												
Utilities												
Miscellaneous												
Total Controllable Expenses												
Fixed Expenses Depreciation												
Insurance												
Rent												
Taxes and licenses												
Loan payments												
Total Fixed Expenses												
TOTAL EXPENSES												
NET PROFIT (LOSS) (before taxes)												

CASH FLOW PROJECTIONS

A cash flow projection is a forcast of the cash (checks or money orders) a business anticipates receiving and disbursing during the course of a month. Well managed, the cash flow should be sufficient to meet the cash requirements for the following month.

CASH FLOW PROJECTIONS

	Start-up or prior to loan	Month 1	Month 2	Month 3	Month 4	Month 5	Month 6	Month 7	Month 8	Month 9	Month 10	Month 11	Month 12	TOTAL
Cash (beginning of month														
Cash on hand														
Cash in bank														
Cash in investments														
Total Cash														
Income (during month)														
Cash sales														
Credit sales payment														
Investment income														
Loans														
Other cash income														
Total Income														
TOTAL CASH AND INCOME														
Expenses (during month														
Inventory or new material														
Wages (including owner's)														
Taxes														
Equipment expense														
Overhead														
Selling expense														
Transportation														
Loan repayment														
Other cash expenses														
TOTAL EXPENSES														
CASH FLOW EXCESS (end of month)														
CASH FLOW CUMULATIVE (Monthly)														

Getting Down to Business...

Home Attendant Service

**An Instructional Guide for Creating A Small Business
by Jerre G. Lewis, M.A.
& Leslie D. Renn, M.S.**

Notes _____

Planning a Home Attendant Service

There are many, many small businesses in America. Small businesses can have as few as one worker (the owner) or as many as four workers. A small business owner is "self-employed." Often a whole family works together in a small business.

In this section you will learn about four things involved in planning a home attendant business:

- deciding what the services, customers, and competition will be;

- deciding what personal skills and characteristics are needed to operate this type of business;

- deciding what to do to compete successfully; and

- learning about the legal requirements for running this type of business.

Services, Customers, and Competition

An important step in planning is to decide what services you will offer, who your customers will be, ant what the competition offers.

Services. A home attendant, homemaker, or home health aide works in a client's home performing any combination of the following types of tasks:

- does light housekeeping;

- does light laundry;

- plans and prepares meals, sometimes following a special diet;

- assists client with bathing, with dressing, and with other grooming;

- assists client to move from bed to chair, down stairs, or into a car;

- shops for food and does other errands;

- drives the client to the doctor or other places;

- serves as a companion and chats, plays games, reads aloud, goes for a walk, or shares other activities;

- helps with child or infant care;

- does other household tasks, such as caring for pets or paying the bills; and

- calls or visits to see that the client is all right and does not have emergency needs.

In summary, the home attendant does what is needed to manage the household and to make the customer comfortable. The specific tasks depend on the needs of the client. The home attendant does not do tasks that require nursing skills or heavy housecleaning.

<u>Customers</u>. There are many people who can use the help of a home attendant. The elderly, handicapped, families with children, working people, and sick people all may need assistance in their home.

About 10% of the population is over 65. This percentage is increasing. Many of these older people are able to live on their own with the assistance of a home attendant. Otherwise they would have to live in a convalescent home. Also as more women work, there is an increased need for both temporary and long-term help in the home. Many people would like a home helper. But they often are not able to afford to pay much for the help.

<u>Competition</u>. There are a number of ways that home attendant services can be provided. A person may want a permanent full-time or live-in attendant. Then she or he will often hire a person. Sometimes the person will contact a nursing registry. Some nursing registries fill requests for home attendants both on a temporary and a long-term basis. Nursing registries usually focus on providing health services. They may have a minimum of four hours of service. Some nursing registries are small owner-operated businesses. Others are large companies with branch offices in different communities. Some businesses specialize in providing homemaking services. Often they schedule a homemaker for two hours a day, one or more times a week. It depends on the needs of the customers.

You may plan on providing this type of service. There are other ways to organize the services provided. A person could set up a business to provide meals, to do daily telephone calls, to do errands, or to provide any other specific service that a home attendant often does.

Personal Qualities

You may want to know if you have the personal qualities to run your own business. Below is a description of the personal qualities that you may feel would be important.

- You feel it is important to relate well with people and be sensitive to their needs.

- You want to be patient and reasonable in dealing both with the customers and your employees.

- You know you must have a balance between wanting to care for people and wanting to make money to stay in business.

- You know you must be organized and pay attention to details for the business to run smoothly.

- You know it will take hard work to start and maintain your business.

Background and experience that would be helpful to the owner of a home attendant business include: home economics, administration, accounting, personnel, social work, counseling, gerontology, public health, disabilities, and related fields. There is no set list of requirements for running a home attendant business. The useful skills can be acquired in various ways.

How to Compete Successfully

There are several things you can do to compete successfully. We will mention them now. You will learn more about them as you study this module.

- Do a lot of research and planning before you start. This will help you decide what services to offer and where to offer them.

- Strive to keep your business expenses low and¡ the quality of your services high. You should offer a service that people want at a price they can afford.

- Establish a business image that people will remember. You will want to be professional, yet friendly.

Legal Requirements

Legal requirements vary according to the types of services you offer and where you are located. You will probably need a local business license. You may need to be bonded. This means you guarantee to pay up to a certain amount in claims against you. Your staff will probably need to meet certain health requirements. These include a TB check or a physical examination. Also there may be local certification programs, such as a certification for a home health aide. To find out what the legal requirements are in your area contact the Department of Consumer Affairs or the Department of Health.

There are other legal requirements to think of when home attendant services can be paid for through medical insurance, government programs and workers' compensation. It is helpful to the home attendant service if some of the costs of the service can be paid for through such sources. Often nursing services are covered, but home attendant services are not. The business owner must check on the current legal requirements.

Summary

There is a need for home attendants to provide light housekeeping, cooking, and personal assistance to elderly, disabled, and ill people. As the number of aged increases, the demand for this service will grow. An owner of a home attendant service should care about people and also have good business sense.

UNIT 2

Choosing a Location

Goal: To help you choose a location for your business.

Objective 1: List three things to think about in deciding on a service area for your business.

Objective 2: Pick the best office location for a home attendant business from three choices.

Notes _____

Choosing a Location

There are several things to think about when you choose a service area for your business and decide what services you will offer. You should consider:

- Are there enough customers in the area?

- What is the competition?

- Is this where you want to work?

You also need to decide on a location for your office. Things to think about are:

- Is the space appropriate?

- Can I afford the rent?

- Is the location convenient for job applicants?

- Does the building reflect the image I want?

- Does the location help in attracting customers?

Customers

Your customers are elderly or other people who want help in the home. They have money to pay for this service. Likely customers would be people who have just been released from a hospital. Other possibilities are elderly people who do not have family or friends to care for them.

Some way to do market research for a home attendant service could include the following.

- Contact the county or city planning department and get information on: the number of people in an area, the age distribution, the income level, and trends in neighborhoods. Some neighborhoods may have a high percentage of older people. But they may be too poor to afford the service. Another area may have strong family traditions where older people are cared for by their family.

- Talk to hospital discharge workers who arrange for the release of people leaving the hospital. Ask them if they know of a need for home attendant services.

- Look in the classified section of the newspaper to see if people are advertising for home help.

- Talk to administrators at convalescent homes, senior centers, churches, and social service agencies about the need for home services.

Competition

Nursing registries usually provide home attendant services. Also some of the temporary employment agencies provide people to do these services. Many people have jobs as home attendants and do not work through an agency.

A home attendant service can compete by offering more personalized attention or flexible scheduling. You may plan to specialize in long-term home attendant service for a few hours a week. One person may want someone to come daily for two hours. Another customer wants someone to come twice a week for three hours. You may plan to establish a service flexible enough to meet these needs. You may also plan on providing short-term, all-day service for people returning from the hospital or who had other emergency needs.

Balance Between Customers and Competition

What is important is the number of customers in relationship to the people offering the service. A big city may have a dozen home attendant services and have more business than they can handle. A small town may not have enough people to support even one such service. So it is important to consider both supply and demand.

Personal Considerations

There are other things to consider about the location. You might ask, "Is this where I want to work? Is this where I want to start a business?" People often have personal reasons, such as friends or family, for deciding where to start their business.

Selecting an Office Location

The office should be in a convenient location. Home attendants will come to the office for their initial interview. Later they may stop by while they are working. They should have easy access to the office. Sometimes the office location can attract customers. They may rarely visit the office. But there might be an advantage to be near a hospital or in a neighborhood where there is a strong demand for your service.

The office itself should have a reception area and a private conference space, for interviews or discussions. The office does not need to be fancy. But it should be clean, neat, and attractive. The building should be in good condition. Also you must be able to afford the rent.

If you intend to hire no employees and sell only your own services, you can work from your home.

Summary

Once you have decided to open a home attendant business, you must research the need for services. You must find out who else provides these services. Your office should be professional in appearance and convenient for your staff.

Notes _____

Being in Charge

Working with your employees is an important part of a home attendant service. The success of your business depends on doing a good job of "being in charge." If you do not have enough attendants, you won't be able to serve your customers. If your attendants do poor work, you may lose business.

In this unit you will learn about:

- tasks involved in running a home attendant service;

- hiring staff; and

- keeping employees happy.

Tasks

Here are major types of tasks involved in operating a home attendant business.

Customer relations. This involves talking to customers on the phone and discussing their needs and available services. Sometimes you must visit a customer's home to learn about their particular situation. You must also handle customer problems.

Employee relations. This area includes interviewing, hiring, training, and supervising employees.

Scheduling. To match customer needs with employee availability requires an effective scheduling system.

Promotion. This involves calling and visiting potential referral sources. You also will prepare newspaper and other advertisements.

Office tasks. There are many such tasks including typing, answering telephone calls, bookkeeping, filing, billing, and record keeping.

Business management. This involves such tasks as setting up systems, establishing policies, reviewing financial records, making business decisions, keeping informed of regulations and requirements, and preparing tax returns.

In a small agency one person may do all these tasks you can plan on running your business. In a larger agency, staff would specialize in the tasks they would do. Specific jobs might include: coordinator, interviewer, secretary, business manager, bookkeeper, or supervisor. Most agencies use an answering service to take messages when the office is closed.

Selecting Staff

To select a good employee, you should be clear on what tasks you want the home attendant to do. You should recruit people who have the skills, experience, and desire to do the job.

Some qualities you might look for include the following:

- enjoys working with the elderly;

- enjoys helping others and is caring and sensitive;

- skill and experience in home management and personal care;

- able and willing to do some heavy physical work;

- does not mind doing housework;

- good health;

- enjoys change and the lack of a set routine;

- reliable;

- dependable car and car insurance;

- telephone at home where can be reached;

- willing to work in neighborhoods where customers live; and

- 18 years of age.

In some areas there is a certificate for a home attendant. It shows that the person has received certain training. Helpful classes would include first aid, gerontology, nutrition, and home economics. A high school degree is not usually necessary. But some basic English skills are important.

Good potential employees include both men and women of all ages. Often women from 40 to 60 years of age work in this field. College students are also good prospects. Often they can work full-time during the summer and part-time during the rest of the year.

Some ways to advertise for home attendants include:

- want ads in local newspapers;

- employment office;

- adult education programs;

- college employment office;

- referrals from current employees; and

- churches, social agencies, etc.

Ads in the classified section of the newspaper can reach a large number of people at a reasonable rate. Also home attendants will often look in the Yellow Pages of the telephone book when they are looking for work. Some agencies put up posters and distribute fliers. Sometimes they offer their staff a bonus of around $25 if they refer a friend who is hired. You will need to find out what the best way is to recruit people in your local area.

It is important to carefully screen job applicants. You want to send well-qualified, dependable home attendants out to customers. Applicants should:

- fill out a job application;

- have a personal interview; and

- provide personal references.

Recent job experience is particularly helpful. It shows that the applicant has done this kind of work and knows what is involved. The personal interview is very important. It can reveal personal qualities that do not show up in an application. Good judgment in interviewing can avoid staff problems later. The applicants' references should be checked out. Often a new employee is hired on a probationary basis for the first three months. Then the employee is evaluated for satisfactory service .

Employee Satisfaction

Once you have hired your home attendants, it is important to do things to keep them happy. You want them to do quality work and continue on the job. You don't want them to quit or have to be fired. Then you will have to spend time and money finding and training new employees. Some of the ways a to keep employees happy are to provide good pay and benefits, clear policies, and appropriate training and supervision.

Pay. The pay you give your employees should be close to what they would get working for someone else. If you pay less, they may get a job elsewhere. If you pay much more, you may not be able to keep your prices low enough to be competitive. You also need to consider benefits. Typical ones a are health insurance, sick leave, and vacation. You can increase the pay rate with length of service to encourage experienced attendants to stay with your agency. A bonus or other money incentive can be used as a reward for work well done.

Clear policies. You should be clear on what your policies are and provide them to employees in written form. Include such things as how assignments are made, how to fill out a time card, when the attendant will be paid, travel allowances, and work duties.

Training and supervision. It is important to train new employees in your procedures. The amount of training required will depend on the experience and skills of the employee. The training can combine office orientation and on-the-job instruction by an experienced worker. There should also be on-going training and supervision to teach improved procedures and to discuss problems. Some agencies have their attendants meet together once a month to share experiences with each other.

Being a home attendant can be hard. The person he or she is caring for may be depressed or irritable. Sometimes the home attendant needs emotional support. He or she needs someone to talk to and provide ideas for dealing with a difficult client. A good supervisor can provide this kind of support and encouragement when it is needed. The supervisor can also recognize work well done to promote a positive work attitude.

Summary

There are many tasks to be done to manage a home attendant business. An owner can do many of these tasks or hire other people to do them. Hiring good employees is critical for the success of the business and should be done carefully. The owner's goal should be to develop a group of dedicated, competent employees who get satisfaction from their work.

Organizing the Work

The major service of a home attendant business is matching up people who want help in their home with home attendants who can provide this assistance. This requires good coordination. A home attendant business must develop a record keeping system. Such a system keeps track of the people available to do the work, the work to be done, when it will be done, and if it gets done as scheduled. This unit gives some samples of the types of forms that can be used in a record keeping system. The sample forms include the most important information. Actual forms used by a business would probably be more detailed.

Keeping Track of the Staff

Keeping a brief summary of each employee and his or her general availability is important. Here is an example of one form you may develop. It includes information on each employee's availability and work preferences. You may keep this information on 5 x 7 inch cards and keep them in a file box on your desk.

Name: _____

Certification: Yes _____   No _____

Availability:

	MON	TUE	WED	THU	FRI	SAT	SUN
Day							
Evening							
24-hour live-in							

Preferences:

Day	_____	Personal Care	_____
Evening	_____	Assist in Movement	_____
Live-in	_____	House Cleaning	_____
Elderly	_____	Meal Preparation	_____
Ill	_____	Driving	_____
Child Care	_____	Companion	_____
Disabled	_____		

You also have a notebook in which you keep the attendant's job application and a form with information on the attendant's status with the agency. In addition, attendants call the office once a week to confirm that they are available.

The Work to Be Done

A work order is used to record the customer's order. The work order is filled out by the owner or another employee after talking to the customer and finding out what service he or she needs. A copy of the work order form is given to the attendant who is assigned that customer.

A sample of the form you may develop appears on the next page.

WORK ORDER

Name _____ Date _____

Address _____ Number _____

Phone _____ Order taken by _____

Client's Condition (physical and emotional) _____

_____

_____

Members in Family	**Age**	**Situation**
_____	_____	_____
_____	_____	_____
_____	_____	_____
_____	_____	_____

Job Description

Personal Care:

Bath _____

Shampoo _____

Shave _____

Shower _____

Assist in Movement:

In bed: turn, etc. _____

Transfer-bed to chair _____

Assist walking _____

Meal Preparation:

Meal planning _____

Meal preparation _____

Special diet _____

Other _____

_____

House Cleaning:

Change bed _____

Vacuum _____

Bathroom _____

Kitchen _____

Laundry _____

Other _____

_____

Driving:

Food shopping _____

Errands _____

Transportation _____

Companion:

Interests _____

_____

Days _____ Starting Date _____

Hours per Day _____ Length of Job _____

Physician _____ Phone _____

Travel Directions _____

_____

The form had a second page with information on the referral source and how to bill for the service.

Scheduling

Scheduling involves matching attendants with work orders. To select appropriate attendants for specific jobs, you would consider their time availability; their skills, experience, and preferences; and how far they are willing to travel. Scheduling for full-day and live-in assignments is generally straightforward. Scheduling becomes more complicated when you schedule part days. You have to consider the attendant's other assignments and the travel time required between assignments. Below is the form you may use for scheduling.

June 1-5

Staff Person	Monday	Tuesday	Wednesday	Thursday	Friday
	8-10 Rush	9-12 Harris	8-10 Rush	9-12 Harris	8-10 Rush
JANE	10-12 Hayes	1-4 Jones	10-12 Hayes	1-4 Franklin	10-12 Hayes
	1-5 Allan		1-5 Allan		1-5 Allan

The home attendant, Jane, shared her time among six different households during the week. She visited them once, twice, or three times.

Time Card

You also have your employees fill out a weekly time card for each customer. The attendant has the customer sign the card. This information is used for paying the attendant and for billing the customer.

TIME CARD

Client:_____

Address:_____

Day	Date	Time In	Time Out	Daily Total of Hours Worked
Monday				
Tuesday				
Wednesday				
Thursday				
Friday				
Saturday				
Sunday				

TOTAL HOURS FOR WEEK: _____

Employee Signature: _____

Client Signature: _____

Time Planning

A major problem for most small business owners is planning their own time. One way to plan is to list all the things you want to do. Then rank them in order of importance. Take into consideration both how important they are to do and when they should be done. Then you can set up a tentative schedule, allowing time for dealing with unexpected tasks during the day.

Summary

A smoothly operating home attendant business depends on an effective system of keeping track of the work to be done and who is doing the work. Then customer requests can be handled quickly and efficiently and attendants will be certain of their assignments.

Notes _____

Setting Prices

To be successful, you must set rates which are acceptable to your customers, are competitive with similar services, and allow for a profit. This unit discusses what to consider in setting rates.

Acceptable to Customers

Your rates must be acceptable to your customers. Many people would like to have a home attendant, but cannot afford it. If the cost of home attendant service is too high, customers will do without it. Or they will find other alternatives. They might use a nursing home, move in with a relative, or find some other source of help.

In Line with Competition

Customers usually check the rates of several services before deciding on one. The clients will not be willing to pay higher prices unless there are extra services or advantages for them, such as reliability or friendly staff. Your strategy is to offer lower prices for partial-day service to be competitive.

Components of Price

Operating expenses. Operating expenses include salaries and benefits. They also include overhead expenses such as rent, utilities, telephone, advertising, repairs on office equipment, supplies, accountant services, license fees, insurance, travel expenses, and all the other expenses to operate a business. The owner takes all these into consideration before deciding what to charge for a service. The owner tries to keep the expenses down. That way he or she can keep prices down, too.

Profit. The profit is what is left over after all expenses have been paid. The profit includes the owner's salary, income tax, and money to improve the business. You must decide how much profit you can make and whether this is acceptable for you. Many small businesses start out with little or no profit in the first year.

Establishing a Price

There are many issues to be considered in setting rates for a home attendant service. Salaries of attendants are the biggest expense. Questions to be decided are:

- Should all attendants be paid the same, or should some get more for length of service or education?

- How much should be spent on benefits such as health insurance, sick leave, and vacation? Some agencies do not provide such benefits. Others consider their attendants to be permanent, full-time employees, and do provide such benefits.

- Should attendants be paid for travel to jobs or between customers? If so, should it be a set rate or based on actual miles driven?

- What is the policy on paying live-in attendants? Live-in attendants work off and on over a 24-hour period, but generally not over 12 hours in one day.

How these questions are decided determines the cost of the attendants.

There is another set of questions to be answered regarding prices. Some services are more expensive to provide than others. For example, it is less expensive to the business for an attendant to work all day at one place compared to working for several customers. The difference is due to travel time. Home attendant services will usually charge different rates depending on the number of hours worked and whether it is a live-in job. Also, a price needs to be established for mileage if the attendant drives the client somewhere or does errands. The business has a fee schedule explaining the costs for different services.

Of course, the owner must charge the customer more than what is paid to the home attendant. It is typical to charge customers from 30% to 50% more than the home attendants are paid.

<u>Summary</u>

Setting prices depends on the cost to provide the service, customer demand, and the prices of the competition. Some services are more expensive to provide than others. Setting rates requires reaching a balance between charging customers an amount they can afford, paying the attendants a fair wage, and making a profit so the owner will have a living salary and the business can continue to operate.

Keeping Your Business Successful

A business must make a profit to continue. Profit is one way to evaluate the success of a business. However, there are other personal satisfactions for some people in running their own business. This section discusses personal satisfaction, key elements of a successful business, ways to increase profits, and using a profit/loss statement.

Profit and Personal Satisfaction

Many people start a small business hoping to make more money than they did working for someone else. They take a risk by going on their own. Some people make much more money. Some make about the same. Others make less than what they could make working for someone else. (It's possible, too, to lose money.) Different people are satisfied making different amounts of money from their business.

There are other considerations to being a small business owner. Some people like working for themselves. They may enjoy the independence, the challenge, or the chance to make the decisions. They are usually persistent, hard working, and motivated. Other people don't like it, even when their business is profitable. They may not like the worries, responsibility, the long hours, or all the decisions. Operating a small business is certainly not appropriate for everyone. Personal satisfaction may be more important than profit.

Key Elements of a Successful Business

Here are some major points to consider to keep a home attend business successful.

Staff. Competent, dependable staff are needed to provide the service.

Satisfied customers. Satisfied customers are the basis for referrals and repeat business which sustains a business in the long run.

Low expenses. A business must keep expenses low to provide services at a price customers can afford and still make a profit.

Trends. Be aware of trends, such as changing age or income level in the area being served. The trend is for an increasing percentage of the population to be elderly. This will depend on the particular community.

Flexibility. The business must adapt to changing conditions, such as competition or the general economic situation. The business should also be responsive to the changing needs of the customers.

Profit/Loss Statement

A profit/loss statement shows revenue, expenses, and profit during a certain period of time. This information can be helpful in determining how a business is doing and in deciding what changes might be made.

A profit ratio and an expense ratio can be figured from the information on the profit/loss statement. They show the percentage of profit and expenses to sales. They are useful in comparing the performance of a business from year to year. They are figured as follows:

$$\text{Profit Ratio} = \frac{\text{Net Profit}}{\text{Revenues}}$$

$$\text{Expense Ratio} = \frac{\text{Expenses}}{\text{Revenues}}$$

How to Increase Profits

A business owner can increase profits by increasing the amount of money coming in and decreasing expenses. It sounds easy but is often difficult to do!

Some ways to increase revenues include:

- raising prices;

- getting more customers;

- working more efficiently and getting more work done;

- providing different services; and

- specializing in the more profitable services.

Some ways to decrease expenses include:

- limiting pay;

- improving office procedures;

- reducing waste; and

- finding an office with lower rent.

Sometimes it is difficult to reduce expenses much without also reducing the services provided. This may lead to a loss of customers.

SUMMARY

There is a need for home support services for elderly, ill, and disabled. These services include personal care, light housekeeping, meal preparation, shopping, transportation, and companionship. The need for such services will increase as we have more elderly people. However, people must be willing to pay home attendants a good wage to attract and keep them on the job.

Some home services are provided by businesses. Some are provided by government programs. Some are provided by non-profit organizations. Sometimes a government agency will pay a business or non-profit organization to provide the service. Businesses that provide home attendants include agencies specializing in home attendants, nurses registries, and temporary employment companies. Some are small owner-operated firms. Others are branches of large organizations.

A home attendant business must strike a balance between taking care of the needs of the customer, being fair to employees, and maintaining a profitable business. To be successful the owner should plan ahead, be organized, enjoy managing other people, make wise financial decisions, and be flexible.

In order to own and operate a successful home attendant business you need training in home economics, work experience, and the special business management skills we have covered in this module. If you have not taken a course in home economics, you may want to take one before deciding to own a home attendant business. You can learn business management skills through business classes, experience, or by using the advice and example of an expert.

Starting your own home attendant business can be a rewarding challenge. Many people like working for themselves. They like the possibility of earning more income than if they worked for someone else. But it takes hard work. It can be risky to start your own business. It is not appropriate for everyone. Think about how important these things are to you in considering whether you should start your own home attendant business someday.

Appendix D

INSURANCE CHECKLIST

TYPE OF INSURANCE	PURCHASE	DO NOT PURCHASE
PROPERTY INSURANCE:		
Fire	_____	_____
Windstorm	_____	_____
Hail	_____	_____
Smoke	_____	_____
Explosion	_____	_____
Vandalism	_____	_____
Water Damage	_____	_____
Glass	_____	_____
LIABILITY INSURANCE	_____	_____
WORKERS' COMPENSATION	_____	_____
BUSINESS INTERRUPTION	_____	_____
DISHONESTY:		
Fidelity	_____	_____
Robbery	_____	_____
Burglary	_____	_____
Comprehensive	_____	_____
PERSONAL:		
Health	_____	_____
Life	_____	_____
Key Personnel	_____	_____

Special Appendix

Web Site Marketing

Business Web Site
an
Effective Marketing Tool

More than 100 million people use the Internet each day. A website offers help in marketing your small business. Your web site can help level the playing field for small businesses who compete with big businesses. It can enable small business to expand their business nationally or internationally.

What makes a good web site?

A good web site shows by doing; it proves rather than states. Instead of making claims, it provides evidence.

Evidence can take several forms:

- Case Studies showing how your efforts solved a previous client's problems.

- Testimonials from satisfied clients.

- Reprints of articles you've written or reviews of your work.

Education, however, remains the best way to establish credibility. To the extent prospects leave your web site better informed about your product or service, the easier it is to gain their respect (and their purchase order).

Three steps to creating your own business web site.

Today's tools make web publishing accessible to small businesses without programming experience. For example, Microsoft® Publisher 97 includes PageWizard design assistants, web deign elements and design checkers to help your build a workable web site.

Step one:

Choose a structure and a look. Your site should be structured and designed to best tell your story. But where do you start? Using the Page Wizard, you can choose from pre-designed options that can later be customized so that establishing a structure and "look" is easy.

Step two:

Tell your story. Next, simply select the sample headlines and text provided and replace them with words that describe what you have to offer.

Step three:

Check your work and post your site. The design in Publisher 97 goes through your web site element by element, identifying potential problems. Then, the web publishing wizard guides you through the process of posting your web site on the local Internet service provider or on-line service of your choice.

Remember, with millions of web sites, you may have to market your web site as well as your small business to get traffic for your business. The web site can be an inexpensive way of effectively building your small business.

10 tips for Web Site Online Marketing

1. Put up a simple web page.
2. Use a name that will attract people
3. Give away advice and information
4. Have lots of e-mail correspondence
5. Provide customized pages for users.
6. Visit user groups
7. Get on mailing lists
8. Arrange links with related sites
9. Make sure you're in every possible directory
10. Do not "SPAM"

INDEX

Step-by-Step Guides
To Start, Manage & Market
Your Own Business

4th Printing!

New!

3rd Printing!

HOW TO START & MANAGE YOUR OWN BUSINESS

A Practical Way To Start Your Own Business

Jerre G. Lewis and Leslie D. Renn

How to Start & Manage a Home Based Business

A Practical Way to Start Your Own Business

by

Jerre G. Lewis and Leslie D. Renn

HOW TO START A PARTICIPATIVE MANAGEMENT PROGRAM

10 EASY STEPS

Jerre G. Lewis and Leslie D. Renn

How To Start & Manage Your Own Business

For anyone who is looking to start-up a new business, this **step-by-step guide** includes planning, managing, marketing and promotion.

$21.95

Soft Cover • 104 Pages
5 1/2" x 8 1/2" 0-9628759-0-2 ©1992

How to Start & Manage a Home Based Business

This book provides the knowledge and tools necessary to successfully plan, design, and start up a new business in a practical way. With a step-by-step guide for planning, managing, marketing and promotion of a small business, in an easy-to-read and easy-to-understand format. The guidelines presented will help you pursue dreams of independence and financial success.

$21.95

Soft Cover • 135 Pages
5 1/2" x 8 1/2" 1-887005-11-0 © 1996

How To Start A Participative Management Program

A concise guide for small to midsize companies that is easy to read and follow. *Step-by-step planning, managing and marketing of a small business* • How to empower and involve employees Contains tools for measuring employee work environment.

$21.9

Soft Cover • 93 Pages •
5 1/2" x 8 1/2", 0-9628759 ©1992

ABOUT THE AUTHORS
Jerre G. Lewis and Leslie D. Renn are both experienced professionals concerning small business management and entrepreneurship. For more than twenty years Mr. Lewis has been involved with business education at college level and the development of a series of small business seminars. He is a Certified Education Specialist for the U.S. Small Business Administration Volunteer Counseling Program. Mr. Renn is a business owner, entrepreneur, a small business consultant, and like Mr. Lewis, is involved with college level management instruction & business seminars. He also has extensive experience in large industry administration. Mr. Lewis and Mr. Renn received bachelors and masters degrees from Michigan universities, and both work and live in northern Michigan.

TO ORDER BUSINESS PLANS

Please Remit To:

LEWIS AND RENN ASSOCIATES
10315 HARMONY DRIVE
INTERLOCHEN, MICHIGAN 49643

Business Book # _____ Title _____

Business Book # _____ Title _____

Name _____

Address _____

City _____

State _____ Zip _____

Business Book _____

U.S. Shipping & Postage $ 3.00

Total _____

Business Books

phone 1-231-275-7287 • Fax 1-231-275-7242 • lewisjv@centurytel.net
phone 1-480-807-9530 • Fax 1-480-830-1187 • lrenn@cox.net

w to Start and Manage:

978-1-57916-152-1 An Apparel Store Business
978-1-57916-153-8 A Word Processing Service Business
978-1-57916-154-5 A Garden Center Business
978-1-57916-155-2 A Hair Styling Shop Business
978-1-57916-156-9 A Bicycle Shop Business
978-1-57916-157-6 A Travel Agency Business
978-1-57916-158-3 An Answering Service Business
978-1-57916-159-0 A Health Spa Business
978-1-57916-160-6 A Restaurant Business
978-1-57916-161-3 A Specialty Food Store Business
978-1-57916-162-0 A Welding Business
978-1-57916-163-7 A Day Care Center Business
978-1-57916-164-4 A Flower and Plant Store Business
978-1-57916-165-1 A Construction Electrician Business
978-1-57916-166-8 A Housecleaning Service Business
978-1-57916-167-5 A Nursing Service Business
978-1-57916-168-2 A Bookkeeping Service Business
978-1-57916-169-9 A Bed and Breakfast Business
978-1-57916-170-5 A Secretarial Service Business
978-1-57916-171-2 An Energy Specialist Business
978-1-57916-172-9 A Guard Service Business
978-1-57916-173-6 A Software Design Business
978-1-57916-174-3 An Air Conditioning & Heating Business
978-1-57916-175-0 A Plumbing Service Business
978-1-57916-176-7 A Sewing Service Business
978-1-57916-177-4 A Carpentry Service Business
978-1-57916-178-1 A Home Attendent Service Business
978-1-57916-179-8 A Tree Service Business
978-1-57916-180-4 A Dairy Farming Business
978-1-57916-181-1 A Farm Equipment Repair Service Business
978-1-57916-182-8 A Children's Clothing Store Business
978-1-57916-183-5 A Women's Apparel Store
978-1-57916-184-2 A Convenience Food Store Business
978-1-57916-185-9 A Pest Control Service Business
978-1-57916-186-6 A Printing Business
978-1-57916-187-3 An Ice Cream Business
978-1-57916-188-0 A Mail Order Business
978-1-57916-189-7 A Bookstore Business
978-1-57916-190-3 A Home Furnishing Business
978-1-57916-191-0 A Retail Florist Business
978-1-57916-192-7 A Radio-Television Repair Shop Business
978-1-57916-193-4 A Dry Cleaning Business
978-1-57916-194-1 A Hardware Store Business
978-1-57916-195-8 A Marine Retailing Business
978-1-57916-196-5 An Office Products Business
978-1-57916-197-2 A Pharmacy Business
978-1-57916-198-9 A Fish Farming Business
978-1-57916-199-6 A Personal Referral Service Business
978-1-57916-200-9 A Solar Energy Business
978-1-57916-201-6 A Building Service Contracting Business
978-1-57916-202-3 A Retail Decorating Products Business
978-1-57916-203-0 A Sporting Goods Store Business
978-1-57916-204-7 A Retail Grocery Store
978-1-57916-205-4 A Cosmetology Business
978-1-57916-206-1 A Franchised Business
978-1-57916-207-8 An Electronics Industry Consulting Practice Business
978-1-57916-208-5 An Independent Consulting Practice Business
978-1-57916-209-2 An Independent Trucking Business
978-1-57916-210-8 An Accounting Service Business
978-1-57916-211-5 A Nursery Business
978-1-57916-212-2 A Seminar Promotion Business

ISBN 978-1-57916-231-9 A Bar & Cocktail Lounge Business
ISBN 978-1-57916-214-6 A Wheelchair Transportation Business
ISBN 978-1-57916-215-3 A Fertilizer and Pesticide Business
ISBN 978-1-57916-216-0 A Desktop Publishing Business
ISBN 978-1-57916-217-7 A Crime Prevention Business
ISBN 978-1-57916-218-4 A Gift Shop Business
ISBN 978-1-57916-219-1 A Handcraft Success Business
ISBN 978-1-57916-220-7 A Coin-Operated Laundries Business
ISBN 978-1-57916-221-4 A Property Management Business
ISBN 978-1-57916-222-1 An Auto Supply Store Business
ISBN 978-1-57916-223-8 A Men's Apparel Store Business
ISBN 978-1-57916-224-5 A Temporary Help Service Business
ISBN 978-1-57916-225-2 An Advertising Agency Business
ISBN 978-1-57916-226-9 A Firewood Sales Business
ISBN 978-1-57916-227-6 A Children's Bookstore Business
ISBN 978-1-57916-228-3 A Used Bookstore Business
ISBN 978-1-57916-229-0 A Sandwich Shop Deli Business
ISBN 978-1-57916-230-6 An Instant Print/Copy Shop
ISBN 978-1-57916-231-3 A Gift Specialty Store Business
ISBN 978-1-57916-232-0 A Gift Basket Service Business
ISBN 978-1-57916-233-7 A Hospitality Management Business
ISBN 978-1-57916-234-4 A Hotel Business
ISBN 978-1-57916-235-1 A Catering Service Business
ISBN 978-1-57916-236-8 A Carpet-Cleaning Service Business
ISBN 978-1-57916-237-5 A Window-Washing Service Business
ISBN 978-1-57916-238-2 An Innkeeping Service Business
ISBN 978-1-57916-239-9 An Apartment Preparation Service
ISBN 978-1-57916-240-5 A Kiosks and Cart Business
ISBN 978-1-57916-241-2 A Janitorial Service Business
ISBN 978-1-57916-242-9 A Medical Claims Processing Business
ISBN 978-1-57916-243-6 A Nursing Home Care Business
ISBN 978-1-57916-244-3 A Home Health Care Business
ISBN 978-1-57916-245-0 A Referral Services Business
ISBN 978-1-57916-246-7 A Hair Styling Salon Business
ISBN 978-1-57916-247-4 A Child Care Service Business

How-To Business Books

ISBN 978-1-57916-248-1 How to Buy and Sell A Business
ISBN 978-1-57916-249-8 How to Advertise A Small Business
ISBN 978-1-57916-250-4 How to Write A Successful Business Plan
ISBN 978-1-57916-251-1 How to Finance Your Business for the 21st Century
ISBN 978-1-57916-252-8 How to Market Your Business for the 21st Century
ISBN 978-1-57916-152-1 How to Start & Manage Your Own Business
ISBN 978-1-57916-152-1 How to Start & Manage a Home Based Business
ISBN 978-1-57916-152-1 How to Start a Participative Management Program

To Order Business Plans

Please Remit To:
Lewis & Renn Associates
10315 Harmony Drive
Interlochen, Michigan 49643

ISBN # _____ Title _____

ISBN # _____ Title _____

Name _____

Address _____

City _____

State _____ Zip _____

Business Book _____

U.S. Shipping & Postage **$ 3.00**

Total _____

Library Discount - 20%
Retail Discount - 20%
$3.00 Postage & Handling
$21.95 Each
www.smallbusbooks.com